Law, Democracy and the Crisis of Foundation

This book addresses the crisis of the juridical-political foundation within contemporary democracies.

Although modernity is the age of foundation, it is marked by what Carl Schmitt referred to as a peculiar 'dialectic of presence and absence' – and this is true even for those theories that seem to be the greatest supporters of the necessity of some kind of foundation, such as the Hobbesian commonwealth. This instability of foundation is inherent in the concept of 'political representation', which brings into being an idea – such as that of 'nation', 'people' or 'popular will' – which cannot, however, actually correspond to any empirical reality. Is it possible, then, to identify an absolute, certain and stable foundation capable of generating and guaranteeing the persistence of a legal and political structure? Or does this very question bind us to the history of an impossibility: a foundational absence, or void, whose presence is only now being strongly felt? Engaging both historical and contemporary perspectives, this book addresses the problem of foundation through both deconstructive and constructive perspectives – which respectively aim to challenge the very idea of foundation, or to overcome its contemporary crisis in order to present new, post-foundational possibilities.

This book will be of interest to scholars and researchers working in the areas of legal and political theory.

Giuditta Bissiato is PhD in Philosophy at the Universities of Pisa and Florence, Italy.

Part of the
Law and Politics: Continental Perspectives
Series

Series editors
Mariano Croce
Sapienza University of Rome, Italy
Marco Goldoni
University of Glasgow, UK

A GlassHouse book

for information about the series and details of previous and forthcoming titles, see https://www.routledge.com/law/series/LPCP

Law, Democracy and the Crisis of Foundation

Deconstructive and Constructive Perspectives

Edited by Giuditta Bissiato

Routledge
Taylor & Francis Group
a GlassHouse Book

First published 2025
by Routledge
4 Park Square, Milton Park, Abingdon, Oxon OX14 4RN

and by Routledge
605 Third Avenue, New York, NY 10158

Routledge is an imprint of the Taylor & Francis Group, an informa business
A GlassHouse book

British Library Cataloguing-in-Publication Data
A catalogue record for this book is available from the British Library

ISBN: 978-1-032-74816-0 (hbk)
ISBN: 978-1-032-74817-7 (pbk)
ISBN: 978-1-003-47106-6 (ebk)

DOI: 10.4324/9781003471066

Typeset in Times New Roman
by Apex CoVantage, LLC

Contents

About the Contributors

Giuditta Bissiato is Ph.D. in Philosophy at the Universities of Pisa and Florence (Italy). Her research interests include political theology, political representation, Hobbesian commonwealth theory, and the relationship between politics and spatiality.

Giacomo Brioni is Ph.D. in Philosophy at the Universities of Pisa and Florence (Italy). His research interests include the history of contemporary classical liberal and libertarian thought, as well as the work of Leo Strauss on classical and modern political philosophy (especially his interpretations of Xenophon and Locke).

Jacopo Marchetti, Ph.D., is Post-Doctoral Fellow at the University of Pisa (Italy). His research interests include political epistemology and information disorders, as well as a philosophical analysis of the cognitive failures of the democratic public.

Francesca Monateri, Ph.D., is Post-Doctoral Fellow at Istituto Italiano per gli Studi Storici of Naples (Italy). Her research interests include Italian contemporary philosophy and the history of the interpretation of the 'katechon' from the Latin Patristic to the twentieth-century debate.

Antonino Scalone, Ph.D., is Associate Professor of Institutions of Public Law at the University of Padua (Italy), where he teaches History of Public Law and Transformation of Welfare States and Social Rights. He is a member of the Political Concepts Research Group of the Department of Philosophy at the University of Padua.

Introduction

Giuditta Bissiato

It is a widespread opinion that a juridical-political order must be based on certain principles in order to be long-lasting and to guarantee peace and security for citizens. More specifically, it is commonly believed that the juridical and political dimensions – though not synonymous, are always interconnected – cannot function properly without a grounding in principles. For example, it seems impossible to produce laws without considering what "justice" means, since any law must be regarded as "just" by citizens to be respected. This idea is also present in the thought of Thomas Hobbes, who, in *Leviathan* (1651), highlights the relationship between justice and sovereignty, asserting that everything enacted by the sovereign must be considered "just" because the sovereign acts as an "artificial person", representing the will of the creators of the covenant (see Hobbes 1651: 99–100), that is, the human beings who form the Commonwealth. The underlying reason is that the obedience of the subjects to the laws requires a shared conception of justice. Without such a shared understanding of justice, it would be impossible to ensure the subjects' obedience to the laws and, consequently, their peaceful existence within the Commonwealth.

Moreover, every democratic system is grounded in the idea of "the people", and governments make political decisions by appealing to this idea. However, this idea is problematic: it can never fully correspond to the personal interests of either politicians or citizens since it transcends both. In the *Glossarium* Carl Schmitt explains this aspect by quoting Goethe: 'Eine idee tritt als ein fremder Gast in der Erscheinung [an idea enters the phenomenon as a foreign guest]' (Schmitt 1991: 211). In other words, an idea like "the people" (*das Volk*) is always foreign to both the representative and the represented (the citizens), due to its ideal nature, which prevents it from fully entering into reality.

At the same time, this idea must be embodied, that is, be represented, in order to produce and maintain a juridical and political order within a democratic system. As Chantal Mouffe (2000: 56) notes:

> Democratic politics does not consist in the moment when a fully constituted people exercises its rule. The moment of rule is indissociable from the

DOI: 10.4324/9781003471066-1

> very struggle about the definition of the people, about the constitution of its identity. Such an identity, however, can never be fully constituted, and it can exist only through multiple and competing forms of *identifications*.

In short, the need to identify principles as the ground of an order always grapples with their ideal nature, that is, the impossibility of fully realizing them in empirical reality.

As suggested by the title of this book, the primary focus is on the issue of juridical-political foundations in democracy, specifically the challenge of discovering an authentic and stable ground for democratic systems. The plurality of perspectives offered by the various contributions aims to do justice to the complexity of this issue, recognizing it as an intricate process centered on the need to establish a lasting order. This process raises troubling questions, such as the possibility of identifying an absolute, certain, and stable ground on which to build a structure that can guarantee its preservation. While many thinkers of previous centuries assumed the existence of such foundation, the ground they identified often revealed itself as an abyss, an absence, or a void.

This sense of void is particularly acute today, likely because we are confronted with numerous crises in a wide array of fields. As Gavin Rae (2016: 1) notes in *The Problem of Political Foundations in Carl Schmitt and Emmanuel Levinas*,

> rather than simply assume a fixed foundation that delineates and legitimizes one conception of the political, the questioning of foundations inherent to contemporary thinking has brought to the fore the need to re-think the political in a way that does not depend on or re-affirm the foundations that previously grounded though.

If we do not acknowledge that there may not be a stable ground, we cannot recognize the limitations of the democratic environment (see Mouffe 2005: 1–2), particularly that of liberal democracy (see Mouffe 2000: 80). In this case, we may mistakenly believe that we live within "the best" juridical and political system, which could block critical reflection on it. In short, the aim is not to dismiss the advantages of living in a democratic system, but to recognize its possible limitations and attempt to find ways to overcome them.

To answer this and other questions, as well as to address issues related to the problem of foundation, this book adopts a philosophical-political approach. This means that, even when drawing on concepts and methodologies from other fields, the goal remains to offer a juridical and political explanation of the crisis of foundation. Such an explanation may require analyzing political concepts, such as "representation", which are central to both law and politics, since both legislation and political decisions are understood as dependent on a representative. The choice to anchor the contributions within the context of the Modern Age, beginning with Hobbes, acknowledges the significance of that age in shaping our contemporary conceptions of law and politics. Indeed, living in a liberal-democratic context, it is difficult for us to imagine abandoning the representative system, which makes abstract ideas, like that that of "the people", visible and present.

Furthermore, this book addresses the issue of foundation – that is, the problematic quest for a stable ground – through two different perspectives that have been recently applied to political theory. Despite their differing views on the possibility of grounding law and politics, both perspectives share a common concern: the need to determine whether a foundation is even possible.

The so-called "anti-foundational" perspective calls into question the idea of law and politics having a stable ground by adopting a deconstructive approach. According to *Post-Foundational Political Thought: Political Difference in Nancy, Lefort, Badiou and Laclau* by Oliver Marchart (2007: 14), the anti-foundationalist approach to political theory assumes 'the absence of *any* ground', meaning the impossibility of finding a ground to justify the existence of law and politics. Consequently, anti-foundationalism critiques the idea of "foundation" by grasping its shortcomings *via* genealogical investigations and exploring the possibility of abandoning it altogether.

Although the Modern Age is often regarded as the "the age of foundation", because modern thinkers sought a certain ground for law and politics, often appealing to human reason, the crisis of foundation arises from its inherently aporetic character. This is true even for political theories, like Hobbes' one, which seem to be the most ardent proponents of some form of foundation. Indeed, as mentioned earlier, Hobbes views the covenant as the origin of the Commonwealth, emphasizing humanity's ability to understand reasonably the need for political power to maintain peace.

If we accept the Hobbesian concept of "representation" as developed in *Leviathan* (Chapter XVI, *Of Persons, Authors, and Things Personated*) as the core of modern political thought and modern democracy, we must acknowledge the instability of the modern attempt to found law and politics. Representation gives presence and visibility to an idea (see Schmitt 1928: 243), such as that of "nation", "people", "political unity", and "popular will", but this idea can never truly correspond to the elements of empirical reality. This non-correspondence between the idea and the empirical complicates the search for a ground for law and politics, since it leaves open the possibility that individuals may resist decision made by the representative, even they are told they do not have the right to do so. For instance, revolution, which challenges the existing order, cannot be accepted by the representative without negating itself.

Even though the second perspective also acknowledges the aporetic nature of foundation, it seeks to approach the issue through a "post-foundational" lens. Unlike anti-foundationalism, which is often deconstructive, post-foundationalism is constructive, offering an alternative way to think about the foundation of law and politics. Rather than denying the existence of any ground, post-foundationalism negates the notion of '*an ultimate* ground, since it is only on the basis of such absence that grounds, in the plural, are possible', so that 'the problem is therefore posed not in terms of *no* foundations (the logic of all-or-nothing), but in terms of *contingent* foundations' (Marchart 2007: 14; see Wingenbach 2016: 5). This means that post-foundationalism accepts the impossibility of discovering an ultimate ground as a means to highlight the crucial role of contingency in the production of laws and political decisions.

According to *Institutionalizing Agonistic Democracy. Post-foundationalism and Political Liberalism* by Ed Wingenbach (2016: 12),

> the task of post-foundational political theory is not to destroy foundations but to make their contingency visible so that politics can incorporate into its regular practice ongoing interrogation, contestation, and re-formation of the necessary but always necessarily incomplete and inadequate grounds of social and political like.

Thus, post-foundationalism does not deny the existence of a ground, but rather challenges the idea of finding a definitive, unchanging one. Post-foundationalism emphasizes the exposure of contingency, which everyone can recognize in the daily dynamics of social and political life, rather than relying on distant, abstract ideas that are harder to grasp.

To register both perspectives, the book engages with key thinkers from different, sometimes opposing, currents of thought. The aim is to demonstrate the continuity and persistence of the question of foundation across these various approaches, highlighting its centrality since the Modern Age. The thinkers discussed here do not simply reflect on democratic systems, such as modern democracy and liberal democracy, but also examine their structural problems. They do not seek to embrace the democratic system as it exists, nor to accept it uncritically, but instead aim to analyze it in a way that could lead to improvements.

In this regard, the decision not to divide the book into two separate parts stems from the desire to allow each contribution to examine, in its own way, the contradictions inherent in the legal and political foundations. If the book were split into distinct sections, it could risk confining each contribution to a single perspective, either anti-foundationalist and post-foundationalist. Instead, the book seeks to highlight how each contribution offers a different facet of a shared field of discussion.

The choice to begin with the contribution *Democracy without Foundation* by Antonino Scalone is connected to its "deconstructive" character. Scalone does not seek to challenge democracy *per se*, but rather to question the idea of "democracy" as a stable political system by analyzing certain aspects of Hobbes' political theory, as well as features of contemporary constitution, such as the Weimar Constitution and the Italian Constitution. By grounding itself on the concept of "the people", which is a transcendent idea that must always be represented, democratic systems reveal their structural contradictions. These contradictions do not eliminate the risk of crisis, but rather contain it. This crisis arises because, even when individuals do not directly participate in juridical and political matters, they may still disagree with decisions made by the political power and thus seek to act as "the people" themselves. On the one side, the idea of "the people" can be seen as ground of all democratic systems, but, on the other, it carries the potential to undermine those systems due to its inability to correspond to any empirical subject.

Scalone's examination of the possibility for individuals to form protest groups, in contrast to Hobbes' denial of the right of resistance, suggests an anti-foundationalist stance. According to Wingenbach (2016: 7), 'for the anti-foundationalist, . . . the role of political theory is to expose the artifice of narratives in order to permit the emergence of resistance and creativity' since 'foundational claims are always hostile to difference and thus always incompatible with emancipation'. However, the contribution by Scalone cannot be fully reduced to an anti-foundationalist approach because its purpose is to analyze the crisis of foundation from a different angle. Beginning with his work allows the book to demonstrate that reflections on the issue of foundation can move beyond the positions articulated by thinkers like Butler, Marchart, Mouffe, Wingenbach, and Rae.

The contribution *The People is Nowhere Here: Political Representation Without Foundation* by Giuditta Bissiato is closely related to Scalone's work, as both begin with Hobbes' thought. However, Bissiato adopts an approach which is not merely deconstructive but also constructive. She delves deeper into Schmitt's concept of "representation" (*Repräsentation*), revealing its contradictory relationship between the representative, the idea being represented, and the individual. Moreover, Bissiato introduces the perspectives of Michel Foucault and especially Judith Butler as alternative ways of thinking about politics. She also argues that both Schmitt's and Butler's approaches engage the issue of foundation, but in different ways. While neither denies the existence of a ground, they both challenge the possibility of finding it once and for all and emphasize the role of contingency.

The contribution *Ironic Law? A new Foundation from Schmittian Romanticism* by Francesca Monateri connects the previous two by analyzing Schmitt's reflection on Romanticism to explain his views of law and politics. After exploring Schmitt's interest in narratives and satires, Monateri outlines three possible interpretations of his position within the crisis foundationalism of the twentieth century. The first interpretation links Schmitt to Martin Heidegger, highlighting the deconstructive aspect of the Schmittian thought and the absence of an ultimate ground. The second aligns Schmitt with Friedrich Nietzsche to emphasize his nihilism. The third perspective, which Monateri champions, sees Schmitt as a romantic figure, reading romantic irony as a "bridge" between legitimation and foundation in both aesthetic and juridical terms. The irony is proposed as a "foundational" narrative form, offering a new way to understand foundation in the literary and political spheres.

As all three contributions give significant importance to Schmitt in their analysis of the crisis of foundation, they underscore the need to expand upon Marchart's reflection, engaging with a range of authors he discusses, including Schmitt, Butler, and Heidegger. For instance, the contribution by Bissiato does not focus on Schmitt's distinction between "the political" (*das Politische*) and politics (*die Politik*) (see Mouffe 2005: 8–34), which Monateri explores, nor on Schmittian political theology (see Rae 2016: 8), though the concept of *Repräsentation* can be interpreted as central to Schmitt's political theology (see Duso 2007: 175).

The same philosophical intention, though developed along a slightly different path, underlies the contribution *Public Choice and Post-Foundationalism: Constitutions, Democracy, and Economic Rationality* by Giacomo Brioni. He compares post-foundational outlook with key tenets of the economic theory of democracy, developed in the second half of the twentieth century by such authors as Anthony Downs, William H. Riker, James M. Buchanan, and Gordon Tullock. Although the latter perspective is often considered at odds with post-foundationalism, Brioni points out that they share methodological similarities when tested within the framework of positive political theory. He shows that this comparison is fruitful, as it highlights the weaknesses of the normative projects in both theories: Buchanan's constitutional political economy and radical democracy.

Finally, the contribution *The Crisis of Foundation and Democratic Representation: A Behavioral Perspective* by Jacopo Marchetti interprets the post-foundational critique through the lens of behavioral theory to understand both social order and democratic institutions, particularly in relation to the crisis of representation. Marchetti identifies unexpected affinities between the post-foundational critique of legal and political institutions and the social philosophy of the Austrian School. He also identifies a *trait d'union* between the latter and subsequent developments in behavioral economics. His aim is to propose the behavioral approach as a mean to address some of the unresolved issues in post-foundational critiques, demonstrating that legal institutions and social norms can emerge from how social agents interpret their world. Within this framework, a behavioral approach suggests that institutions should be grounded in the interests, preferences, and behaviors of real people, using evidence and experimental settings to provide a more comprehensive understanding of the factors influencing individual and collective decision-making.

The idea of this book emerged from the international conference *The Crisis of Foundation: Metaphysics, Epistemology, Politics*, held in Pisa on December 12–13, 2022. The conference was organized by Ph.D. students at the University of Pisa. I am grateful to my colleagues Claudio Davini and Nicola Ramazzotto, as our research interests differed, yet we managed to organize this event and discuss the common theme of the crisis of foundation.

The panel *Politics and Democracy* – the other two panels addressed epistemology and metaphysics – brought to identify a gap in the literature. I aim to fill this gap with this collective volume, which focuses on the crisis of foundation from both juridical and political perspectives. Although I was aware of the complexity of engaging with such a diverse range of authors, who, as mentioned earlier, belong to sometimes opposing currents of thought, I was confident that we could produce a work in which these differing perspectives would be fully respected, while also illustrating their connection to the central topic of the crisis of foundation.

I must express my gratitude to Giacomo Brioni, who, in addition to his excellent work as chair of the panel *Politics and Democracy*, was a crucial collaborator in this project from the start. I also thank the other authors for their contributions: Antonino Scalone, who accepted the challenge of tackling familiar arguments from new perspectives; Jacopo Marchetti and Francesca Monateri, who, like Scalone, embraced this project as a challenge for their research interests.

Bibliography

Duso, G. (2007) *La logica del potere: Storia concettuale come filosofia politica*, Monza: Polimetrica International Scientific Publisher.

Hobbes, T. (1651) *Leviathan or the Matter, Forme, and Power of a Common-Wealth Ecclesiasticall and Civill*, London: Andrew Coke.

Marchart, O. (2007) *Post-Foundational Political Thought: Political Difference in Nancy, Lefort, Badiou and Laclau*, Edinburgh: Edinburgh University Press.

Mouffe, C. (2000) *The Democratic Paradox*, London and New York: Verso.

Mouffe, C. (2005) *On the Political*, London and New York: Routledge.

Rae, G. (2016) *The Problem of Political Foundations in Carl Schmitt and Emmanuel Levinas*, Palgrave Macmillan.

Schmitt, C. (1928) *Constitutional Theory*, Durham and London: Duke University Press, 2008.

Schmitt, C. (1991) *Glossario*, Milano: Giuffrè, 2001.

Wingenbach, E. (2016) *Institutionalizing Agonistic Democracy: Post-Foundationalism and Political Liberalism*, London and New York: Routledge.

1 Democracy without Foundation

Antonino Scalone

1. The Crisis of Democracy: People and Sovereignty

The thesis under scrutiny posits that modern democracy is characterized by a fundamental contradiction. Rather than being the result of a gradual decay or a transformation of democracy among the centuries, this contradiction is inherent in the origins of modern political thought. While many authors address the perceived crisis and the decline of the state, we should confine our preliminary discussion to two illustrative examples: Carl Schmitt and Santi Romano. In his 1963 *Foreword* to *The Concept of the Political* Schmitt (2015: 20) states:

> The era of statehood is now coming to an end. . . . The state as the model of political unity, the state as the bearer of the most astonishing of all monopolies, namely the monopoly of political decision, this gem of European form and occidental rationalism, is dethroned.

In *The Modern State and its Crisis* Romano (see 1909: 29) not only asserts the state's incapacity to adapt to social transformations but also highlights the crisis of political representation, pointing to the proliferation of organizations of interests, such as trade unions. Thus, we aim to show the intrinsic structural connection between the concept of the (democratic) "state" and the concept of "crisis ab origine", that is, the idea of the modern state as a "crisis-state".

1.1. To support this thesis, we must consider the ideas developed by Thomas Hobbes, since modern political thought, including the concept of "democracy", finds its origins in his philosophy. In this regard, Hobbes conceived the notion of "absolute power" – and democracy *is* an absolute power – as emerging from a mechanism of authorization. The absoluteness of power derives its authorization from below, that is, the will of the contracting parties. Consequently, except in exceptional circumstances, which we will examine later, the "right of resistance" becomes implausible, since it is contradictory to resist a power one has contributed to establish, and to which one has delegated certain functions.

DOI: 10.4324/9781003471066-2

Within the Hobbesian framework, the notion of "the people" cannot be regarded as a starting point, but rather as an endpoint because, instead of wielding power, it is the result of the mechanism that produces it. In essence, "the people" is not an actual presence, but an idea (see Leibholz 1966: 25–43; Schmitt 2008: 239–248; Pitkin 1972: 14–37) that needs to be made present, that is, represented by a "person", a group of people, or an assembly. For this reason, in Chapter XVI of *Leviathan*, Hobbes (1996: 114) writes:

> A multitude of men are made one person, when they are by one man, or one person, represented. . . . For it is the unity of the representer, not the unity of the represented, that maketh the person one. And it is the representer that bereth the person, and the person one: and unity cannot otherwise be understood in multitude.

Furthermore, there is a structural and ineradicable distinction between the representative and the represented, which makes it fundamental for the represented to place their trust in the representative to make the system function and govern this distinction. Specifically, there must be confidence in the representative's capacity to articulate and realize the common interest and the popular will. On the one hand, this trust is eroding in contemporary political systems, thereby engendering a structural deficit of legitimacy. On the other, modern political systems rest upon the trust of the represented in their representatives. As this trust diminishes, so does the stability of the political system. In any case, this erosion of trust is inevitable as individual expectations diverge from the common good, and they tend to organize themselves around shared needs to advance their interests. Trust in representatives is further undermined when individuals perceive them as incapable of making optimal decisions due to their susceptibility to the influence of powerful group of interests.

1.2. Evidently, the legitimacy deficit of democracy does not derive from its decay or transformation, but rather from the very structure of the concept itself. Since "the people" – the bedrock of legitimacy – is not constituted at the outset, because it emerges only at the end of the process of authorization, it is untenable to state that the democratic system is adequately founded. Using Kelsenian terminology, a transfer of powers and competencies from "the people" to the legislative and governing bodies cannot be fully demonstrated (see Kelsen 1925). Indeed, in *The Essence and Value of Democracy*, Hans Kelsen (2013: 50) discusses the 'fiction of representation', whose purpose is to 'legitimize parliamentarism from the standpoint of popular sovereignty'. Therefore, parliamentarism represents a compromise between the democratic imperative for freedom and the division of labor, which is the essential basis for all progress in social technique (see Kelsen 2013: 49).

The term "compromise" is pivotal in Kelsen's conception of "democracy". Firstly, it justifies parliamentarism, notwithstanding the shortcomings of this system acknowledged by Kelsen, who devotes several pages of his essay to such deficiencies. Secondly, "compromise" is the inevitable and desirable outcome of political contention, as party actions ought to aim at reaching a mutually beneficial compromise rather than a utopian common good, whereas brandishing the banner of the common good is just a mean of better pursuing one's own interests while denying those of the others. In short, political power does not come from below. However, individuals must *recognize themselves* as authors of the political order and identify themselves with the decisions of the sovereign.

If individuals find that their expectations are not satisfied and their interests unaddressed, they may gain the power necessary to dissolve the existing social contract and establish a new one. In this way, the modern conception of "politics" embraces the *jus revolutionis*. Moreover, existing order has no transcendental value, as it persists and endures insofar it upholds the terms of the covenant, by guaranteeing human life for *every* member. As a result, even if the right of resistance is circumscribed to exceptional circumstances, it characterizes and conditions the entire structure of the constituted power.

More specifically, the "right of resistance" demarcates the insurmountable limit of political power, which, irrespective of its absoluteness, remains purely instrumental to the interests of individuals who fashion it through the covenant[1]. It is intriguing to note that, even if the Lockean individualistic framework is less stringent compared to the Hobbesian one, Locke is often regarded as a liberal thinker. His philosophy permits the withdrawal of trust by the Commonwealth from the government without necessitating the dissolution of the covenant and the return to a pre-contractual state. Moreover, the Commonwealth reserves the right to demand that individuals sacrifice their lives for the defence of the common good. In *The Second Treatise of Government* (XI, 134) Locke (1960: 355–356) posits: 'The *first and fundamental natural Law*, which is to govern even the Legislative itself, is *the preservation of the*

1 On the right to resistance in Hobbes see Finkelstein 2001: 358; Sreedhar 2010: 136. The former interprets it as 'a natural right of revolution'; the latter writes: 'I argue that there is an identifiable and coherent Hobbesian right of rebellion and, moreover, I argue that this right is consistent with Hobbes's stated rejection of rebellion in the cases that he addresses'. Schmitt' interpretation is diametrically opposed. Indeed, Schmitt (1996: 46) writes: 'Resistance as a "right" is in Hobbes' absolute State . . . is factually and legally nonsensical and absurd. . . . There are no points of departure for a right to resist, irrespective of whether it be an objective or a subjective right. It has no place whatsoever in the space governed by the irresistible and overpowering huge machine of the state. It has no starting point, location and viewpoint: it is "utopian" in the true sense of that word'.

Society, and (as far as will consist with the public good) of every person in it'. In short, grounded in Hobbes' thought, the political dimension is circumscribed by the private dimension, with the private individuals serving as the arbiter.

Thus, the private individual receives public dignity, while political power remains grounded in individual interests, since its dimension is the repository of the private one. To better explain this, we can say that political power is generated to guarantee peace and security to individuals; in other words, it must ensure to the contracting parties the possibility to pursue freely their personal projects of happiness. These parties authorize sovereignty to act in their name and on their behalf. On the one hand, they remain judges of sovereignty's actions; on the other, they must obey the commands of the sovereign as expressed through the form of the law. Individuals owe external obedience, whereas in the internal forum they retain the right to think as they wish. This is exemplified by the belief in miracles. According to Hobbes, subjects must believe in miracles in public because the sovereign requires it, even if they hold different belief privately.

As Schmitt notes, this produces an almost imperceptible "crack" in the power of the "great Leviathan", which becomes bigger over the centuries, by making the public opinion derive from private freedom of judgement. Public opinion claims to judge political power because it must serve individuals and their interests. Thus, the public sphere and the private sphere are inextricably connected, with the former ultimately dependent on the latter.

In *The Leviathan in the State Theory of Thomas Hobbes*, Schmitt (1996: 55–56) writes:

> But at this place, at the zenith of the sovereign power that brings about the unity of religion and politics, occurs the rupture of the otherwise so complete, so overpowering unity, the decisive point, concerning miracle and belief, that Hobbes evades. Regarding the question of the belief in miracles, he made his non-eradicable, individualistic proviso in a way that renders any discussion of whether he was an "individualistic" superfluous for our considerations.

By dealing with freedom of thought regarding miracles, Hobbes produced 'the seed of death that destroyed the mighty Leviathan from within and brought about the end of mortal god' (Schmitt 1996: 57). However, Schmitt acknowledges that the death of the mortal god is a necessary consequence of Hobbes' consistent individualism[2].

2 In the final chapter of the *Leviathan*, in the name of freedom of conscience, Hobbes introduces a further limitation of sovereign power. As Quentin Skinner has noted, this is an important innovation compared to the earlier works, such as *Elements* and *De Cive*. In fact, in these two works Hobbes 'strongly denies that subjects have any right to determine for themselves the meaning

Reinhart Koselleck well illustrates this aspect by picking up on and developing Schmitt's analysis. Koselleck (1988: 37) writes:

> Hobbes's man is fractured, split into private and public halves: his actions are totally subject to the law of the land while his mind remains free, "in secret free". From here on the individual is free to migrate into his state of mind without being responsible for it.

As the tragic memory of the religious civil wars fades, the space of private opinion inevitably tends to expand, claiming to bring politics under its scrutiny. Therefore, to all intents and purposes, private opinion becomes a political subject itself, namely "public opinion". Koselleck (1988: 39) states:

> The authority of conscience remained an unconquered remnant of the state of nature, protruding into the formally perfected State. . . . To the extent to which the initial situation, the religious civil war to which this State owed its existence and its form, was forgotten, raison d'état looked like downright immorality.

The neutralization of religious conflicts (*Silete theologi in munere alieno!*) allows to produce a political order that, on the one hand, is completely secularized but, on the other, can be judged by those who made the social contract. In the development and progressive politicization of private opinions, Schmitt sees an intolerable limitation of sovereignty, which becomes powerless due to the proliferation of parties and organizations of interests that paralyze it by undermining the unity of the state. This is precisely what happened during the Weimar Republic, so that a social system was torn apart by crossed vetoes of the parties and on the brink of civil war. During this period, Schmitt wants to support the concentration of power in the hands of the Reich President (see Scalone 2020: 83–118). However, Schmitt also recognizes the impossibility of sterilizing public opinion, since, in *Constitutional Theory*, he defines it as 'the modern type of *acclamatio*' (Schmitt 2008: 275). Rather than being unitary, public opinion consists of parties, organizations of interests, etc., meaning it cannot be fully institutionalized. Schmitt (2008: 275) writes: 'Public opinion arises and exists in an "unorganized" form'. In short, he believes

of the scriptures or what they enjoin by way of worship' (Skinner 2008: 168). However, in the *Leviathan* Hobbes (1996: 479) states that today 'we are reduced reduced to the Independency of the Primitive Christians to follow Paul, or Cephas, or Apollos, every man as he liketh best'. Hobbes adds immediately afterwards, in a passage that Skinner (2008: 168) judges 'quiet but extraordinary', 'which . . . is perhaps the best' (Hobbes 1996: 479–480). This means, concludes Skinner (2008: 169), that 'not only does he applaud the increase of freedom attendant on the defeat of episcopacy as well as presbyterianism; he explicitly speaks in favour of the arrangement under which everyone is left at liberty to formulate their religious beliefs according to the dictates of conscience, subject only to the civil power'.

organizations of parties and interests are, on the one hand, a danger for the maintenance of political unity but, on the other, a constituent element of it.

> Within certain limits, this plural opinion performs an essential political function, through which public opinion cannot be fully institutionalized because it always remains free and indeterminate. Moreover, public opinion cannot be separated from the concepts of "freedom of the press" and "freedom of expression", which reveal a specifically political importance. In fact, Schmitt (2008: 277) states: 'The use of press freedom and freedom of expression of political opinion is not only engagement inside the private sphere of freedom. It is also public activity, the exercise of a certain public function that constitutes public control'.

1.3. We argue that modern political systems are characterized by a "dual tension". The first tension concerns the relationship between the freedom of individuals and the political power. On the one hand, individuals freely make a social pact to achieve peace and security by authorizing the sovereign to decide on their behalf. On the other hand, in doing so, they establish a power that inevitably limits their freedom. The second tension concerns the fact that, by taking advantage of the peace and security guaranteed by the sovereign, individuals tend to associate in groups of various kinds to pursue their own interests. In doing so, they weaken the political power they built up.

In this regard, after dealing with the freedom of subjects in Chapter XXI of *Leviathan*, Hobbes devotes Chapter XXII entirely to the description and classification of such associations. Some scholars trace this back to Hobbes' realism (see Bobbio 1989: 171), suggesting that he sometimes deviates from his rigid rationalistic framework to take historical reality into account, thus making his theoretical proposal more realistic. More convincingly, other scholars focus on the radical individualism that drives the entire Hobbesian logic, specifically the assumption that, if one assumes the contract between free individuals as the foundation of the state, one cannot exclude, in principle, the constitution of other associations (see Gierke 1954: 355).

In any case, this dual tension gives to modern political systems not only their dynamic character but also an incomplete physiognomy. In our opinion, we can find both these aspects in the Weimar Constitution, as well as in many post–World War II European Constitutions, such as the German *Grundgesetz* and the Italian Constitution.

2. Individuality and Plurality

These constitutions can be defined as "pluralistic" because, instead of denying the plurality of political subjects, they tend to enhance the role of these subjects. Indeed, each subject – parties, organizations of interests, trade unions, associations, etc. – has the right and duty to pursue not only its own interests but also the interests of its members. Rather than being the expression of an imaginary common good, the "law" coincides with the compromise between different organized interests and political point of views. As we can easily see, this is a conception of politics that corresponds in many aspects to what Kelsen theorizes in *The Essence and Value of Democracy*.

2.1. In any case, the Weimar Constitution is based on a series of preliminary compromises, the most important of which is the so-called *Legien-Stinnes Pact*, signed on November 15th, 1918, between organizations of workers and employers. As consequence of this pact, the Constitutional Charter gives an ample space to the protection of workers and their rights, to the freedom of trade union association, to the contractual equality between workers and employers, and to the mandatory nature of the national employment contract. Moreover, the system of representation of workers is constitutionally recognized (Article 165), especially through the *Reichswirtschaftsrat*.

Although Article 165 remains largely unimplemented, it expresses a point of non-return in the acknowledgement of the political relevance of the social partners and of the political role of workers as "workers". Even if only mentioned once in the constitutional text, parties are recognized as essential elements in the political will-forming process, as well as an insurance against any demagogic drift (see Thoma 1929: 105).

2.2. The pluralistic character of post–World War II federal Germany is due to two elements. First, according to Article 20, the definition of Germany as a "welfare state" (*Sozialstaat*) gives to the social partners and organizations of interests an essential role in social planning and economic programming procedures. This article acknowledges the political role of workers and their organizations, as well as a way to control social conflicts by integrating workers into the life of institutions.

Second, the role of parties in the political will-forming process is fully recognized. For example, Article 21 establishes that political parties "contribute" (*mitwirken*) to this process. If the acknowledgement of the political role of workers and their organizations also aims at controlling social conflict, the recognition of the institutional role of the parties has the goal to sterilize the influence of the so-called "anti-system parties" (see Ridola 1982: 74; Costa 2012: 75). In this perspective, the distinction between "state" and "civil society" gradually disappears, since the formation of political will does not belong exclusively to either the state or the social sphere; rather, it takes places within a "public" sphere where both spheres intermingle and blur (see Böckenförde 1977: 199–200).

2.3. Going further, the pluralist principle seems to permeate the entire text of the Italian Constitution, even if we will limit our analysis to a few hints. Already in the first part of the text, dedicated to "Fundamental Principles", this principle can be found in Article 2, which deals with "social formations", and in Article 5, which recognizes local autonomies. Furthermore, in the section "Citizens' Rights and Duties", the pluralist principle is at the basis of Article 18, which sanctions freedom of association and gives great importance to the parties, conceived as associations with a special and specific political value (art. 49), and to trade unions.

Trade unions are particularly important because they are one of the consequences of the acknowledgement in the Constitutional Charter of the reality of class differences and the propulsive role of social conflict. Rather than being only a radical break with the principles of the liberal state prior to the advent of fascism and with the approach of the Albertine Statute, this is also a decisive break with the corporatist approach through which the fascist regime claimed to "institutionalize" and authoritatively control organizations of workers.

There is a further aspect of the Italian Constitution that makes it original in comparison with the other constitutions mentioned, that is, the notion of "the people". In the Weimar Constitution and the *Grundgesetz*, sovereignty and power are derived from "the people". However, in the Italian Constitution, sovereignty belongs to "the people", even if it can transfer its exercise to other subjects under certain conditions. This cannot be merely regarded as a lexical difference, for example if we consider that in the Constituent Assembly took place a long and articulated discussion around the term to be adopted. In the end, the choice fell on the term "belongs" to indicate that sovereignty is and remains the exclusive prerogative of "the people" (see Scalone 2021: 126).

In our opinion, this choice is not an isolated one. Limiting ourselves to two recent examples, both the 2008 Ecuadorian Constitution and the 2009 Peruvian Constitution use the verb *reside*, stating that sovereignty *resides* in "the people", which exercises it in various ways, reflecting the plural character of "the people" itself. In short, it should be emphasized that sovereignty *belongs* to "the people" or *resides* in "the people", even though "the people" itself is not a unitary subject but a plural one.

Considering the Italian Constitution, terms such as "social formations", "associations", "local autonomies", "trade unions", and "parties" indicate some of the ways through which "the people" – we could say: the idea of the people – becomes concrete. However, the Constitutional Charter does not provide an exhaustive list of these concretizations of the will of "the people" so as not to contradict the absolute character of sovereignty. As Vezio Crisafulli (1985: 144) notes, ""the people" is 'internally differentiated into smaller classes and groups, bearers of different and conflicting interests'. According to Tommaso Edoardo Frosini (1997: 173), "the people" is not to be understood as a

> politically unitary subject, in whose will is manifested the general interest destined to prevail over any will, but rather as a subject – composed of a multiplicity of individuals, groups, and smaller collectivities – which remains such even after expressing itself unitarily through elections[3].

If the sovereignty of "the people" also depends on the ways and forms it decides to manifest itself, the notion of "sovereignty" of "the people" can never be fully exhausted in the present, especially due to its plural character. As a result, in a democratic system the constituent process can never be concluded because "the people" can never achieve a definitive configuration, and it is always free to manifest itself in new and unprecedented forms and ways.

3. The Concept of the People in Contemporary Constitutions: Open Issues and Provisional Conclusions

The articulated, complex, and never entirely complete notion of "the people" we tried to outline, especially in the context of the Italian Constitution, leads us to some provisional conclusions.

a. If democracy means the "power of the people", and if "the people" is not and cannot be a unitary subject, then the contradiction from which we started cannot be resolved. As we wanted to demonstrate though reference to Hobbes, this contradiction stems from the logic of the modern way of thinking about politics. The concepts of "unity" and "plurality" are not mutually exclusive; in fact, they are mutually implied. Moreover, instead of being a value, political unity is simply the outcome of the pact made between individuals. Therefore, the fulfilment of this pact or the realization of the terms of the contract always depends on the judgement of the

3 From what has been said, the difference between this notion of "people" – plural, articulate, conflictual – and the concept of "nation" should be clear. In fact, the concept of "nation" expresses something substantial, organic, pre-political: it has to do with history, with tradition or presumed tradition, with territorial, linguistic, and ethnic roots. The concept of the "nation" excludes conflict and plurality by definition since the parties must compose themselves into a superior synthesis. Otherwise, they represent an element of disturbance, of instability, and as such must be placed in a condition not to harm in the name of national primacy and national interest. But such a conception seems alien to the logic of the twentieth century constitutional state, i.e., the state that emerged after the end of World War II and the defeat of fascist and national-socialist totalitarianism: the twentieth century Constitutional State is based on a constitutional pact of which the organized parties – primarily the mass political parties – are the architects.

contracting parties, hence on the political importance of public opinion and its plural character, as Schmitt himself recognizes (*obtorto collo!*).

b. The term "people" does not correspond to an empirical reality. Instead, it is an idea that must be represented, namely, to become present. This means that any aggregation of individuals can legitimately claim to represent a substantial and significant portion of "the people". For this reason, parliamentarian type of representation is only one of the possible ways through which "the people" manifests itself. Compared to other models – equally legitimate – this parliamentarian type cannot claim any monopoly over the representation, since it can be completely deprived of different forms of manifestation of the will of "the people". This also means that social and political conflict is not necessarily a danger or a sign of a malfunctioning democracy. If democracy is "the power of the people" and if "the people" is inherently divided, then the conflict between the constituent parts is a symptom of a well-functioning system.
c. Moreover, the constitution-making process never ends. As Thomas Jefferson argues, no constitution can bind future generations. Similarly, the French Declaration of 1793 recites: 'A people always has the right to revise, reform and change its constitution. A generation cannot subject future generations to its laws'. In our opinion, the fascination and enduring vitality of democracy lays in its structural unfoundedness, namely in the fact that it can never be definitively realized. In short, democracy paradoxically seems to draw strength precisely from the aporias underlying its concept.

Bibliography

Bobbio, N. (1989) *Thomas Hobbes*, Torino: Einaudi.

Böckenförde, E.-W. (1977) 'Die Bedeutung der Unterscheidung von Staat und Gesellschaft', in *Staat, Gesellschaft, Freiheit*, Frankfurt a.M.: Suhrkamp, pp. 185–220.

Costa, P. (2012) *Gli istituti di difesa della Costituzione*, Torino: Giappichelli, 2023.

Crisafulli, V. (1985) 'La sovranità popolare nella Costituzione', in *Stato, popolo, governo: Illusioni e delusioni costituzionali*, Milano: Giuffré, pp. 89–156.

Finkelstein, C. (2001) 'A Puzzle About Hobbes on Self-Defense', *Pacific Philosophical Quarterly*, 82, pp. 332–361.

Frosini, T.E. (1997) *Sovranità popolare e costituzionalismo*, Milano: Giuffré.

Gierke, O. (1954) *Das deutsche Genossenschaftsrecht: Vierter Band. Die Staats- und Korporationslehre der Neuzeit*, Graz: Akademische Druck und Verlagsanstalt.

Hobbes, T. (1996) *Leviathan*, Cambridge: Cambridge University Press.

Kelsen, H. (1925) *Allgemeine Staatslehre*, Berlin: Springer.

Kelsen, H. (2013) *The Essence and Value of Democracy*, Lanham: Rowman & Littlefield.

Koselleck, R. (1988) *Critique and Crisis*, Cambridge, MA: MIT Press.

Leibholz, G. (1966) *Das Wesen der Repräsentation und der Gestaltwandel der Demokratie im 20. Jahrhundert*, Berlin: De Gruyter.

Locke, J. (1960) *Two Treatises of Government*, Cambridge: Cambridge University Press.

Pitkin, H.F. (1972) *The Concept of Representation*, Berkley, Los Angeles and London: University of California Press.

Ridola, P. (1982) 'Partiti politici', in *Enciclopedia del diritto 32*, Milano: Giuffré, pp. 66–127.

Romano, S. (1909) *Lo Stato moderno e la sua crisi*, Pisa: Vannucchi.

Scalone, A. (2020) *Percorsi schmittiani*, Milano-Udine: Mimesis.

Scalone, A. (2021) 'Democrazia senza fondamento? La produzione della forma politica e il problema della pluralità', in Carrino, A., Ciampi, M., De Angelis, C., Scalone, A., and Stella, G. (eds.), *Modelli democratici a confronto tra principio di legalità e principio di autorità*, Napoli: Editoriale scientifica, pp. 95–140.

Schmitt, C. (1996) *The Leviathan in The State Theory of Thomas Hobbes*, Westport, CT and London: Greenwood Press.

Schmitt, C. (2008) *Constitutional Theory*, Durham and London: Duke University Press.

Schmitt, C. (2015) *Der Begriff des Politischen*, Berlin: Duncker & Humblot.

Skinner, Q. (2008) *Hobbes and Republican Liberty*, New York: Cambridge University Press.

Sreedhar, S. (2010) *Hobbes on Resistance: Defying the Leviathan*, Cambridge: Cambridge University Press.

Thoma, R. (1929) 'Sinn und Gestaltung des deutschen Parlamentarismus', in Harms, B. (ed.), *Recht und Staat in Neuen Deutschland*, Berlin: Hobbing.

2 The People is Nowhere Here

Political Representation without Foundation

Giuditta Bissiato

1. Rejecting the Natural, Embracing the Artificial

In this contribution, I aim to use modern foundationalism as a starting point for my reflection, particularly the idea of Modern Age as an era of foundations, certainties, and stability. According to Oliver Marchart (see 2007: 13), foundationalism was especially hegemonic during the Modern Age due to rationalistic attempts to conceive the source of law and politics as something certain, measurable, and calculable. Indeed, modern Rationalism seeks to undermine the pre-modern conception of the political order as something fully constituted (see Scalone 2021: 100).

In *Leviathan*, Thomas Hobbes produces a "rupture" with previous thought by criticizing the Aristotelian concept of *zoon politikon* (see Hobbes 1651: 104–106; Piccinini 2009: 127) and arguing that human beings are not naturally sociable, as in nature they are *homini lupus*. Hobbes' thought is a good example of this process, though it does not fully align with Rationalism since it proposes that both passions and reason help humans understand the advantages of living in a *societas civilis* created by a "covenant", through which human beings renounce their 'right of nature' (*jus naturale*), that is, 'the liberty each man hath to use his own power as he will himself for the preservation of his own life' (Hobbes 1651: 79). In short, while the existence of a juridical-political order requires the rejection of everything belonging to nature, nature itself is a hostile place where 'a condition of war of everyone against everyone' prevails (Hobbes 1651: 80).

Hobbes and the most modern rationalist thinkers attempt to ground their political theories on certain principles (see Marchart 2007: 11) and strongly believe in the derivation of politics from human nature. Although there are authors, such as Joseph de Maistre, who argue that it is a mistake to base constitution on human foundations, and that human reason must always rely on God, the "refusal of nature" through human reason can be seen as a characteristic trend of the Modern Age. As I will explain, together with reason, Hobbes' concept of "representation" highlights the problem of foundation, that is, the challenge to find an authentic and stable ground for law and politics.

DOI: 10.4324/9781003471066-3

This problem arises because, on the one hand, the concept of "representation" is the source of order but, on the other, its own features tend to undermine that order.

The examination of the concept of "representation" helps demonstrate that the Modern Age can be interpreted as 'the crisis of the foundationalist horizon' (Marchart 2007: 33), rather than as the age of foundationalism. More specifically, Hobbes' concept of "representation" shows that both juridical and political dimensions are absent in nature, as their existence is contingent upon the sovereign as a 'legislator/creator who exist outside of this naturalistic world' (Rae 2016: 43). Furthermore, sovereignty's task is to produce the "civil laws" that make the "law of nature" (*lex naturalis*) mandatory, ensuring protection for individuals. Thus, the sovereign is an "artificial person", in the sense that 'the person is the actor and he that owneth his words and actions is the author, in which case the actor acteth by authority' (Hobbes 1651: 99; see Wolin 2004: 250).

If political representation derives solely from the human "transfer" of the absolute right to all things to the sovereign's person, the covenant's purpose is 'to elicit from members an acknowledgment of the sovereign's right of way' (Wolin 2004: 254) and to enable the sovereign to prevent the unlimited movements of human beings, which might lead to conflict, thus protecting them as if they were protecting themselves. Therefore, the obedience to the sovereign is due only to his "fictional nature", in the sense that 'for a man to be "obliged" is for him to be bound, to be constrained by some external impediment imposed, directly or indirectly, by himself' (Oakeshott 1975: 69).

Hobbes illustrates the moment of the covenant's stipulation in the frontispiece of the 1651 edition of *Leviathan*, depicting a huge man whose body is composed of a multitude of smaller human figures (see Hobbes 1651: 101). The frontispiece clearly shows that sovereignty controls only the head (thought) and the hands (action) of the huge man (see Farinelli 2009: 80), while the body is divided into two parts, meaning the sovereign does not own his entire body, as it is filled in by smaller humans (see Wolin 2004: 238).

Nevertheless, only the sovereign acts as a single person (see Hobbes 1651: 101), and individuals do not matter politically because they 'agreed to will *not* to act' (Wolin 2004: 254). They must obey his laws, even if they are conceived as a "multitude", 'because the multitude naturally is not one, but many' (Hobbes 1651: 101; see Wolin 2004: 268). In this regard, in *The Leviathan in the State Theory of Thomas Hobbes*, Schmitt (1938: 33) writes: 'The sovereign-representative person, is much more than the sum total of all participating particular wills. . . . To that extent the new god is transcendent vis-à-vis all contractual partners of the covenant and vis-à-vis the sum total'. Thus, human beings become a "multitude" when they stipulate the covenant, that is, when they decide to "extract" themselves from their natural state (see Rosanvallon 1998: 19) and bind themselves to the absolute power of sovereignty.

Within the Commonwealth, individuals are reduced to "atoms" and deprived of their absolute right to all things, and sovereignty is "transcendent" to them, both individually and collectively. This reduction prevents the destruction of the *societas civilis* by avoiding the formation of "indocile subjects" (see Farnesi Camellone 2013: 15, 127), namely, individuals seeking to escape from incorporation within the sovereign's body by appealing to hope. On the one side, hope is a human passion that sovereignty cannot fully contain or control (see Farnesi Camellone 2013: 69), as it means 'appetite with an opinion of attaining' (Hobbes 1651: 34). On the other, sovereignty must prevent hope through two elements: firstly, the production of the civil laws, since 'there is need of the ordinances of sovereign power, and punishments to be ordained for such as shall break them; which ordinances are therefore part of the civil law' (Hobbes 1651: 164); and secondly, two "biopolitical mechanisms" (see Chignola 2021: 19), represented in the frontispiece by the guards and the doctors. These mechanisms convey the need to control the subjects and safeguard not only their health but, most importantly, the health of the entire Commonwealth (see Agamben 2015: 47–48; Bissiato 2022: 73; Chignola 2021: 19; Galli 2017: 150). In brief, alongside civil laws, these mechanisms contribute to the preservation of the Commonwealth.

Hobbes believes only the civil laws exert a "strong hold" on the external world, even though he assigns a fundamental role to the laws of nature in fostering the obedience required to build and sustain the juridical-political order. On the one hand, the laws of nature help human beings recognize the benefits of living in peace, as they correspond to 'qualities that dispose men to peace and to obedience' (Hobbes 1651: 164). On the other, Hobbes (1651: 164) argues that within the "state of nature", the laws of nature 'are not properly laws', since they cannot oblige human beings to act in *foro externo* (see Hobbes 1651: 97). Hobbes (1651: 98) also writes:

> These dictates of reason [the laws of nature] men used to call by the name of laws, but improperly: for they are but conclusions of theorems concerning what conduceth to the conservation and defence of themselves; whereas law, properly, is the word of him that by right hath command over others.

Therefore, the laws of nature cannot be properly regarded as "law" because its existence depends on the sovereign who creates and interprets it (see Oakeshott 1975: 118).

However, Hobbes (1651: 164) appears to reconsider this assumption when he states: 'Civil and natural law are not different kinds, but different parts of law; whereof one part, being written, is called civil and the other unwritten, natural'. Two points emerge from this statement: first of all, as Hobbes (1651: 164) suggests, the laws of nature are a 'part of the civil law in all Commonwealths of the world', while civil laws are 'a part of dictates of nature';

second, both natural and civil laws belong to the same "law", with civil laws making natural dictates mandatory (see Bobbio 1954: 183). In any case, Hobbes believes the human mind is the true source of the Commonwealth-making process and thus the production of the 'artificial chains, called civil laws, which they [human beings] themselves, by mutual covenants, have fastened at one end on the lips of a man, or assembly, to whom they have given the sovereign power, and at the other to their own ears' (Hobbes 1651: 130). Hobbes sets the foundation of the juridical-political order in human mind's capacity to produce order through the construction of the sovereign's person. Thus, Hobbes can be interpreted as a foundationalist thinker.

2. Beginning to Question the Foundation: Political Representation

Nevertheless, Hobbes' assumption of the artificiality of sovereignty makes it difficult to identify an authentic ground for the juridical-political order. Indeed, the potential proliferation of the "indocile subjects" hinders the stability of the artificial person, which lacks "physical density", as it consists of a collective subject that functions only through representation. Consequently, the idea represented by sovereignty cannot be found within empirical reality (see Rosanvallon 1998: 20–22) because it belongs to another dimension of reality. In other words, while it is true that the order is founded through the 'mutual transferring of right' (Hobbes 1651: 82) to the sovereign's person, it is also true that this foundation is "aporetic" due to its representative nature. Therefore, on the one hand, the idea represented can guarantee the juridical-political order insofar as it is incorporated into the body of the sovereign (see Farnesi Camellone 2013: 25) but, on the other, it can never become a part of empirical reality or be fully known.

As Schmitt highlights, representation (*Repräsentation*) creates a gap between the idea represented and what cannot be represented, that is, individuals belonging to empirical reality. Even though Schmitt acknowledges that this gap could destabilize the representative-represented relationship to the point of compromise, he argues that it is necessary to accept the impossibility of overcoming this gap (see Rae 2016: 13–14). Furthermore, Schmitt grasps the "confidence" (*Vertrauen*) (see Rae 2016: 32–33) as an element capable of leading individuals to trust that the representative acts in accordance with the idea embodied, as well as to recognize his superiority as governor. Thus, the representative-represented relationship can only be guaranteed through an irrational element since representation does not cause the idea to lose its original nature.

The fact that the connection between the idea and individuals can only be maintained through confidence further complicates the issue of foundation. By emphasizing the irrational origin of law and politics, Schmitt seeks to undermine the modern rationalist[1] attempt to establish a juridical-political order based on human reason. As Gavin Rae (2016: 32) notes, the essence of Schmitt's "political theology" (*Politische Theologie*) – a concept I cannot delve into here – is to recognize and affirm 'the positive role faith plays in human existence because it recognizes and affirms the limits of human cognition'. In other words, Schmitt's aim is to show that a mediation between the idea and empirical reality is impossible, as there is always an "exception" between them (see Galli 1996: 10). In short, juridical-political order stems from something irreducible to human cognition: an idea whose realization depends solely on the transcendent action of the representative.

As Rae (2016: 46) observes, the Schmittian argument is to link 'faith to transcendence and reason to immanence' in order to show that transcendence involves the impossibility of fully analyzing an object to uncover its truth, as part of it is always withheld from human cognition. If human cognition can only believe that the hidden part of an object is precisely as it thinks it is, human existence becomes a matter of belief rather than knowledge of reality (see Rae 2016: 47). In this regard, in *Constitutional Theory*, Schmitt (1928: 243) writes: 'To represent means to make an invisible being visible and present through a publicly present one. The dialectic of the concept is that the invisible is presupposed as absent and nevertheless is simultaneously [*gleichzeitig*] made present'. Thus, Schmitt seems to interpret the incapacity of representation to establish a perfect correspondence between the idea and empirical reality as a positive aspect, viewing the "tensive dialectic" of representation as maintaining the original features of both elements.

The impossibility of representation overcoming both the idea and empirical reality presents a challenge to foundation rather than its elimination. Despite his efforts to undermine the idea of reason as a grounding principle, and the possibility of fully knowing the ground, Schmitt does not deny that a ground exists. His critique of juridical-political foundation becomes clearer when examining two distinct aspects of the concept of *Repräsentation*. First, representation expresses a contradiction, as the representative can never locate the idea within empirical reality to establish a stable and lasting order. In *The Value of the State and the Significance of the Individual*, Schmitt (1914: 96) seems aware of this limitation when he writes:

> The dignity which he [the sovereign] demands and which is attributed to him applies only to his office and not to be a mortal man [*sterblich Mensch*]. Due to the kind of divine likeness/similarity [*Göttahnlichkeit*] that the absolute monarch has as "living law" [*lebendiges Gesetz*], he is

1 Modern Rationalism is a current of thought that develops between the Fifth and Sixteen century, marking the transition from traditional Christian theology to a system of natural science and the birth of the Enlightenment (see Schmitt 1932: 83, 89). In this context, see also Galli 1996: 3–8, 10.

> immediately subject to the law, like the God of theology, whose omnipotent will cannot want anything evil and non-rational.

Second, and related to this citation, the *body* of the representative not only functions as the *medium* for the embodiment of the idea but also as a limit since it is destined to perish. Therefore, the inevitable change of the representative's body risks undermining the representative-individuals relationship, as individuals may not trust the new governor in the same way they trusted the one who died.

Schmitt's point is that foundation is based on *contingency*, meaning that, from the one side, it must be affirmed to maintain the juridical-political order and, on the other, it involves alterations (see Rae 2016: 30), such as the changing body of the representative. Despite these changes, new governors must demonstrate that their decisions still depend on the same idea to keep the trust of individuals in their embodiment. In this regard, Schmitt (1914: 85) writes: 'The majesty of the state consists in the fact that the effective organization of forces stands above all individual and in its totality employs everyone, even the most powerful despot, as an instrument, since it extends far above him'. Here he considers the state (*Staat*) as the *medium* through which representation can give a concrete reality (*Wirklichkeit*) to the idea of "law" (*Recht*), in the sense that the idea can acquire visibility and presence *within* and *through* the state, even though it remains independent from the law of the state.

Modern Rationalism tends to view the natural body as the site of primordial impulses and generally assigns it little importance since it is associated with physical weaknesses. The negative interpretation of the body as a condition from which human beings should distance themselves is aimed at establishing human reason as the foundation of law and politics (see Butler 2015: 45). For instance, the depiction of a tiny desert city in the frontispiece of *Leviathan* suggests Hobbes' intention to overcome earlier spatial conception by asserting the Commonwealth as the core of law and politics, so that 'the blessings of peace are assured only when society is in total subjection to an absolute authority' (Wolin 2004: 238).

Moreover, Hobbes tends to downplay the natural body, even while acknowledging its existence. When Hobbes (1651: 182) defines the Leviathan as 'that mortal god to which we owe, under the immortal God, our peace and defence', he not only suggests the transcendence of the sovereign but also that his mortality is linked to his being a product of human reason, and his demise can be accelerated by the "indocile subjects". Thus, in *The Leviathan in the State Theory of Thomas Hobbes*, Schmitt (1938: 33) argues that the omnipotence of Hobbes's sovereignty 'is not at all divinely derived' because 'it is a product of human work and comes about because of a "covenant" entered into by man'.

Even in *Behemoth,* where Hobbes addresses the natural body, he assigns it little importance. For example, by emphasizing the political nature of the one who commands, Hobbes (1681: 26) writes that the king 'commands the people in general but never by a precedent law, and as a politic, not a natural person'. From this statement emerge two points: first, the idea that obedience to the king is due to his status as a "political person", meaning his body is a union of both political and natural bodies; second, a reference to the theory of the "two king's bodies", as explained in *The King's Two Bodies* by E.H. Kantorowicz through an examination of medieval theories. Kantorowicz (1957: 9) argues that the political and natural bodies of the king constitute 'one indivisible unit, each being fully contained in the other', meaning that the political body can transcend the imperfection of human nature. In other words, the king's political body is stronger than the natural body, as it 'does not experience "disease"' and can address the 'endless search for a foundation that will support the mass of contradictions present in society' (Wolin 2004: 40). While the union of these two bodies was foundational in the Middle Ages (see Rae 2016: 37), during Modernity it is less emphasized. However, the example of the "Crown" solves the problem of mortality by conveying the capacity to establish temporal continuity, healing the separation between the two bodies.

3. Expanding the Question: The Role of the Body

As mentioned earlier, from Modern Age onwards, most thinkers tend to overlook the fact that the idea embodied by the representative must always contend with the bodily dimension. This leads them to complicate the claims regarding the foundation of law and politics. Nevertheless, some contemporary thinkers, such as Michel Foucault and Judith Butler, emphasize the bodily dimension by challenging this interpretation of politics, which separates the political body from the physical one, in order to maintain the tension between the idea and empirical reality[2].

In *Society Must Be Defended*, Foucault states that the understanding of subject's formation requires focusing on bodies. Criticizing the modern concept of "sovereignty", Foucault (2003: 28–29) writes: 'We should be trying to discover how multiple bodies, forces, energies, matters, desires, thoughts, and so on are gradually, progressively, actually and materially constituted as subjects, or as the subject', that means 'to study the multiple peripherical bodies, the bodies that are constituted as subject by power-effects'. To pursue this objective, in *Discipline and Punish*, Foucault (1995: 221) defines "discipline" as 'the unitary technique by which the body is reduced as a "political" force

2 In this regard, it is helpful to consider that Hannah Arendt and Arendtians, such as Wolin, emphasize the "associate aspect" of politics, that is, the capacity for collective action in the public sphere. This is clearly in contrast to the "dissociative aspect" highlighted by the Schmittian tradition (see Marchart 2007: 39–40), which maintains that it is necessary to preserve the tension between the idea and empirical reality.

at least cost and maximized as a useful force' (Foucault 1995: 221). In short, Foucault (see 1995: 137–138) connects discipline to the human body, believing that discipline can make the body more obedient and useful for society.

Discipline can make the body "docile", meaning that the body 'may be subjected, used, transformed and improved' (Foucault 1995: 136). Moreover, it acts on bodies not only to modify them but also to take the souls they contain 'as an instrument of power through which the body is cultivated and formed' (Butler 1993: 33). In relation to this and to the first volume of *History of Sexuality*, in *Bodies that matter*, Butler (1993: 33) suggests that Foucault understands the 'materialization' of the body by dealing with the body of the prisoner and constructing a 'history of bodies' through the investigation of the materials and vital elements that invest them. Butler suggests that this approach to think about bodies further complicates the issue of foundation, as an order based on bodies must directly confront the problem of their mortality, that is, the problem of *contingency*.

In *Notes Toward a Performative Theory of Assembly*, Butler criticizes Hannah Arendt's assumption of the "pure pre-political character" of the body, which refers to the Christian community as a *corpus* whose members consider each other as a part of the same family (see Arendt 1958: 53). Especially in *On Revolution*, Arendt shows the human body as 'a master signifier of necessity, irresistibility, imitability, and the determination of pure process' (Honig 1992: 217). However, her 'actors are never self-sovereign' because 'driven by the despotism of their bodies (and their psychologies) in the private realm, they are never really in control of what they do in the public realm, either' (Honig 1992: 219). By questioning the tradition that gives centrality to the political body while hiding the natural body within the private sphere, Arendt (1963: 155) states that 'no revolution is even possible where the authority of the body politic is truly intact'.

Furthermore, in *The Human Condition*, Arendt (1958: 72) affirms that 'from the beginning of history to our own time it has always been the bodily part of human experience that needed to be hidden in privacy'. As a result, Arendt proposes 'a participatory conception of politics that calls for an active, performative distinction of a plurality of physically present actors, flesh-and-blood human beings' (Cavarero 2021: 20). Indeed, Arendt defines politics as 'a public sphere of appearance in which human beings, through their interactions with others, distinguish and reveal themselves' (Cavarero 2021: 20).

Arendt believes that, through interaction in shared place, bodies conceived as a 'plurality of embodied uniqueness' can acquire a political status (see Cavarero 2021: 20) and become equal (Cavarero 2021: 21). From her perspective, Butler (see 2015: 127) argues that Arendt is only partially correct when she recognizes the "space of appearance" as a moment of political action, since she does not consider other factors that contribute to the foundation of this space, such as infrastructure and architecture. However, Butler (see 2015: 129) agrees with Arendt's idea of the body embedded within a network of relations, stating that it is impossible to conceive the body both singularly and ideally. The human body can acquire a political meaning and be considered "vulnerable" only if grasped as constitutively relational (see Butler 2015: 130) and in motion.

Butler shares with Hobbes the idea of mobility as a right. Hobbes (see 1651: 80) attributes a central role to mobility (see Maschke 1979: 280) as an expression of liberty, through which human beings can move without encountering obstacles, although this right is ultimately limited by sovereignty. In *Contingent Foundations*, Butler not only deals with the topic of mobility but also adopts a post-foundationalist approach based on "contingency" (see Butler 1992: 7; Marchart 2007: 14). In short, her approach deconstructs the concept of "bodies" without negating it, since the loss of epistemological certainty, which results from the problematization of bodies, 'does not necessarily entail political nihilism as its result' but rather 'provides the condition to *mobilize* the signifier in the service of an alternative production' (Butler 1992: 17).

Again related to the topic of mobility, in *Bodies that matter*, Butler (1993: IX) states: 'Not only did bodies tend to indicate a world beyond themselves, but this movement beyond their own boundaries, a movement of boundary itself, appeared to be quite central to what bodies "are"'; whereas, in *Notes Toward a Performative Theory of Assembly*, Butler (2015: 138) defines mobility as 'a right of the body' and as 'a precondition for the exercise of other right, including the right of assembly itself'. Butler (see 2015: 48) sees the act of assembling as the only way to allow bodies to act freely within the public sphere (see Arendt 1963: 124) and to make them equal to each other, thus addressing the issue of the vertical representative-represented relationship. Through these statements, Butler aims to affirm a 'politics of alliance' which 'rests upon, and requires, an ethics of cohabitation' (Butler 2015: 70).

Going deeper, Butler (see 2015: 71) argues that politics must involve the plurality of bodies in order for them to find their capacity for 'seizing and reconfiguring the matter of material environments'. Nevertheless, Butler (see 2015: 124) does not believe that all politics can be done on the street, nor that mass demonstrations should always be celebrated. This is because Butler (see 2015: 124) does not assume an inherent goodness or badness of bodies but believes in their capacity to take on different values, which strictly depends on what brings them together and how the assembly works.

In *Bodies that matter*, Butler (see 1993: 4) aims to support practices that encourage processes of disidentification, seeking to facilitate a reconceptualization of "the bodies that matter". Going even further back, in *Gender Trouble*, Butler (1990: 194–195) criticizes 'the foundationalist reasoning of identity politics' because it 'tends to assume that an identity must first be in place in order for political interest to be elaborated and, subsequently, political action to be take'. In short, through this critique, Butler (1990: 195) seeks to negate the existence of 'a doer behind the deed', since 'the "doer" is variably constructed in and through the deed'.

As mentioned earlier, Butler also aims to propose a post-foundationalist approach which assumes 'the absence of *an ultimate* ground, since it is only on the basis of such absence that grounds, in the plural, are possible' (Marchart 2007: 14). In *Contingent Foundation*, Butler (1992: 7) writes that 'the point is not to do away with foundations, or even to champion a position that goes under the name of anti-foundationalism' because 'both of those positions belong together as different versions of foundationalism and the skeptical problematic it engenders'. As a result, Butler (1992: 6) states that 'the task is to interrogate what the theoretical move that establishes foundations *authorizes*, and what precisely it excludes or forecloses' since the "foundations" consist in 'premises that function as authorizing grounds'. Therefore, her statement suggests the possibility of thinking about foundation not in the way of rationalist thinkers but rather in terms of contingency.

4. Conclusions

Butler's post-foundationalist approach can be read both in opposition to, and connection with, Schmitt's approach. While both can be classified as post-foundational thinkers, they differ significantly in focus. Butler centers her reflection on plurality, rather than singularity or ideality, while Schmitt seeks to build a community through the *Repräsentation* of an idea. Neither assumes the absence of any foundation – the anti-foundationalist thesis – but rather the impossibility of discovering an ultimate ground (see Marchart 2007: 14; Rae 2016: 29). More specifically, Butler views reality as always open to contingency, whereas Schmitt argues that the source of law and politics cannot be found in empirical reality, as it consists of an idea that must, on the one side, be embodied through representation and, on the other, be trusted by individuals.

Rather than abandoning the search of a ground, Schmitt, too, believes in a foundation based on contingency, suggesting that 'there is a ground to thinking, but that this ground is contingent and changing' (Rae 2016: 29). In short, both interpretations emphasize the need to find a ground to understand how to conceive and maintain the juridical-political order. However, neither offers a complete resolution to of the issue of foundation because their respective focuses are limited: bodies cannot make political decisions on their own, as they require an idea to prevent acting on particular interests, while the idea itself cannot provide a foundation unless it is embodied and trusted.

On the one hand, Schmitt's position is to ground law and politics on the ideal dimension, neglecting the importance of empirical reality. Butler, on the other hand, acknowledges that, although an "alliance of bodies" is crucial for political decisions, it does not entirely constitute politics. In contemporary contexts, Butler's awareness seems more relevant. Political decisions today may be better understood as aiming to embody "plurality", rather than "political unity", by distributing power to allow for a greater representation of differences. Thus, the acknowledgment of the absence of an ultimate ground should be seen not as a negation but as an opportunity to explore new practices and articulate new forms of knowledge.

Bibliography

Accarino, B. (2007) '"Tabula constituens": Tra appropriazione cartografica e geografia politica', in *Confini in disordine: Le trasformazioni dello spazio*, Roma: Manifestolibri, pp. 33–66.

Agamben, G. (2015) *Stasis: Civil War as a Political Paradigm (Homo Sacer II)*, Stanford, CA: Stanford University Press.

Arendt, H. (1958) *The Human Condition*, Chicago and London: The University of Chicago Press.

Arendt, H. (1963) *On Revolution*, London: Penguin Books.

Bissiato, G. (2022) 'Il duplice sguardo del Leviatano: A partire dai frontespizi del Leviatano e del De Cive di Thomas Hobbes', in Angelini, G., Bissiato, G., Capria, A., and Farnesi Camellone, M. (eds.), *Congetture politiche: Scritti in onore di Maurizio Merlo*, Padova: PUP, pp. 65–80.

Bobbio, N. (1954) *Legge naturale e legge civile nella filosofia politica di Hobbes*, Torino: Edizioni Ramella, pp. 61–101.

Bredekamp, H. (2012) *Thomas Hobbes "Der Leviathan": Das Urbild des modernen Staates und seine Gegenbilder, 1651–2001*, Berlin: Akademie Verlag.

Butler, J. (1990) *Gender Trouble: Feminism and the Subversion of Identity*, New York: Routledge.

Butler, J. (1992) 'Contingent Foundations: Feminism and the Question of "Postmodernism"', in Butler, J., and Scott, J.W. (eds.), *Feminists Theorize the Political . . .*, London: Routledge, pp. 3–22.

Butler, J. (1993) *Bodies That Matter: On the Discursive Limits of "Sex"*, London and New York: Routledge.

Butler, J. (2015) *Notes Toward a Performative Theory of Assembly*, Cambridge, MA and London: Harvard University Press.

Cavarero, A. (2021) *Surging Democracy: Notes on Hannah Arendt's Political Thought*, Stanford, CA: Stanford University Press.

Chignola, S. (2019) *Foucault's Politics of Philosophy: Power, Law and Subjectivity*, New York and Oxon: Routledge.

Chignola, S. (2021) 'Homo Homini Tigris: Thomas Hobbes and the Global Images of Sovereignty', *Philosophy and Social Criticism*, pp. 1–29.

Farinelli, F. (2009) *La crisi della ragione cartografica*, Torino: Einaudi.

Farnesi Camellone, M. (2023) *Indocili soggetti. La politica teologica di Thomas Hobbes*, Macerata: Quodlibet.

Foucault, M. (1995) *Discipline and Punish: The Birth of the Prison*, New York: Random House.

Foucault, M. (2003) *"Society Must Be Defended": Lectures at the Collège de France, 1975–76*, New York: Picador.

Galli, C. (1996) *Genealogia della politica: Carl Schmitt e la crisi del pensiero politico moderno*, Bologna: Il Mulino.

Galli, C. (2017) 'Due piccoli medici tra biopolitica e teologia politica: Congetture su un particolare del frontespizio del *Leviatano* di Hobbes', *Schifanoia*, 52–53, pp. 145–151.

Hobbes, T. (1651) *Leviathan or the Matter, Forme, and Power of a Common-Wealth Ecclesiasticall and Civill*, London: Andrew Coke.

Hobbes, T. (1681) *Behemoth: The Long Parliament*, Anodo Books, 2019.

Honig, B. (1992) 'Toward an Antagonistic Feminism: Hannah Arendt and the Politics of Identify', in Butler, J., and Scott, J.W. (eds.) *Feminists Theorize the Political . . .*, London: Routledge, pp. 215–238.

Kantorowicz, E.H. (1957) *The King's Two Bodies: A Study in Medieval Political Theology*, Princeton: Princeton University Press.

Marchart, O. (2007) *Post-Foundational Political Thought: Political Difference in Nancy, Lefort, Badiou and Laclau*, Edinburgh: Edinburgh University Press.

Maschke, G. (1979) 'Der Souverän ist die öffentliche Seele: Der Sterbliche Gott des Thomas Hobbes', *Frankfurter Allgemeine Zeitung* (LAV NRW, RW 0265, NR. 21849).

Nicoletti, M. (1990) *Trascendenza e potere: La teologia politica di Carl Schmitt*, Brescia: Morcelliana.

Oakeshott, M. (1975) *Hobbes on Civil Association*, Indianapolis: Liberty Fund.

Piccinini, M. (2009) 'Potere e rappresentanza in Thomas Hobbes', in Duso, G. (ed.), *Il potere: Per una storia della filosofia politica moderna*, Roma: Carocci, pp. 123–142.

Rae, G. (2016) *The Problem of Political Foundations in Carl Schmitt and Emmanuel Levinas*, Palgrave Macmillan.

Rosanvallon, P. (1998) *Le Peuple introuvable: Historie de la représentation démocratique en France*, Paris: Éditions Gallimard; transl. it. *Il popolo introvabile: Storia della rappresentanza democratica in Francia*, Bologna: Il Mulino, 2005.

Scalone, A. (2021) 'Democrazia senza fondamento? La produzione della forma politica e il problema della pluralità', in Carrino, A., Ciampi, M., De Angelis, C., Scalone, A., and Stella, G. (eds.), *Modelli democratici a confronti tra principio di legalità e principio di autorità*, Napoli: Editoriale Scientifica, pp. 95–140.

Schmitt, C. (1914) *Der Wert des Staates und die Bedeutung des Einzelnen*, Tübingen: J.C.B. Mohr Verlag.

Schmitt, C. (1928) *Constitutional Theory*, Durham and London: Duke University Press, 2008.

Schmitt, C. (1932) *The Concept of the Political*, Chicago and London: The University of Chicago Press, 1996.

Schmitt, C. (1938) *The Leviathan in the State Theory of Thomas Hobbes: Meaning and Failure of a Political Symbol*, Westport, CT and London: Greenwood Press, 1996.

Wolin, R. (2004) *Politics and Vision: Continuity and Innovation in Western Political Thought*, Princeton and Oxford: Princeton University Press.

3 Ironic Law?

A New Foundation from Schmittian Romanticism

Francesca Monateri

1. The Romantic Legacy in Carl Schmitt's Political Thought: An Introduction

Carl Schmitt's position in the crisis of foundationalism in twentieth-century political philosophy is of central importance. Foundationalism, the search for an ultimate and indisputable basis of knowledge, also concerns the question of the necessity of a foundation for legal and political order. From this perspective, Schmitt's position is extremely ambiguous: is Carl Schmitt a foundationalist, anti-foundationalist, or post-foundationalist thinker? Many interpreters are willing to acknowledge Schmitt's challenge to an ultimate foundation. Some interpretations emphasize the deconstructive aspects of Schmitt's thought, drawing him closer to Martin Heidegger and highlighting the absence of an ultimate foundation for the political order. These perspectives suggest that Schmitt's work implies that the political sphere cannot rely on a stable and immutable foundation but must instead recognize the fluid and contingent nature of political legitimacy. This view resonates with Heidegger's critique of metaphysics.

Other interpretations, however, emphasize a sense of nihilism in Schmitt's work, drawing parallels with the philosophy of Friedrich Nietzsche. This approach sees Schmitt as grappling with the implications of a world devoid of absolute values or foundations, where political authority must be established and maintained through power and decision rather than intrinsic legitimacy. Schmitt's concept of the "state of exception", where sovereign power asserts itself beyond legal norms, exemplifies this confrontation with foundational nihilism.

This article proposes a third interpretation through the aesthetic lens. Although often marginalized, aesthetics plays a central role in Carl Schmitt's legal thought. Schmitt perceives aesthetics as offering a possibility for legitimation. This is evident in at least three aspects of his work: 1. his satires, stories, and poems, along with his personal relationships with contemporary artists; 2. his writings on Theodor Däubler's *Nordlicht*, *Hamlet*, and Miguel de Cervantes' masterpiece *Don Quixote*; 3. his interpretation of German

DOI: 10.4324/9781003471066-4

Romanticism as an aesthetic-political movement. Schmitt's interest in aesthetic themes increasingly takes on a political dimension. A key element of Schmittian aesthetics, as I will try to elucidate, is irony, capable of simultaneously highlighting the constructive aspects of his thought and underscoring his ambiguous relationship with German Romanticism. Romantic irony, criticized but embraced by Schmitt, is a bridge between legitimation and foundation. In the legal sphere, Schmitt addresses the tension between the necessity of a stable legal order and the recognition that legal norms are ultimately rooted in political decisions. This dynamic interplay reflects the romantic irony of recognizing the provisional nature of ultimate foundations while seeking a new and coherent order. Politically, Schmitt's engagement with foundationalism highlights the complex relationship between political authority and legitimacy. His work implies that political order is not upheld by an absolute and indisputable foundation, but by the continuous process of legitimation through the exercise of power. Schmitt, through the revival of romantic irony, bridges the gap in the foundationalism debate between deconstruction and construction in political theory.

Three eminent interpreters of Schmittian thought give importance to *Political Romanticism* (1919): first, Hugo Ball, who makes an extensive commentary on political theology; second, Karl Löwith, who writes *Occasional Decisionism* to adopt the Schmittian category of "occasionalism"; third, György Lukács, who carries out a historical-philosophical analysis of German irrationalism (see Ball 1924; Löwith 1935; Lukács 1954). By suggesting a profound relationship between Schmitt and Romanticism, these interpretations go beyond mere exegesis. According to them, this relationship involves parallelism and affinity, rather than contradiction. It's as if Romanticism were Schmitt's *alter ego* by representing a moment of radical self-criticism (see Sombart 1991). In short, if traces of Romanticism persist in Schmittian thought as an unexamined residue, despite his severe critique, it seems that what Schmitt intentionally excludes from his theory remains unintentionally unexpressed.

Political Romanticism embodies Schmitt's struggle with himself, in the sense that it faces the greatest danger of his thought, namely irrationalism, occasionalism, or what Ball and Lukács call *amorphism*. In this contribution, I want to argue that Schmitt and Romanticism are deeply connected because, even if Schmitt does not fully share the lack of foundation he imputes to Romanticism along the lines of Hegel, they both seek a new approach of grounding politics. Indeed, drawing on early Romanticism, on the one hand, Schmitt recognizes the need for an aesthetic answer to the crisis of the modern world. Schmitt sees art as one of the first figures of the *katechon*, that is, as a response to political disorder, to social dissolution. Interestingly, however, according to Schmitt, Romanticism is groundless precisely because of the excessive prominence it would have given to aesthetics as a philosophical discipline. Schmitt is thus a critic and lover of aesthetics, and something similar applies to the Romantic movement. Schmitt is its harshest critic, even if he does not distance himself completely from the purpose of early Romanticism. For this reason, I do believe in the importance of understanding which aspects of Romanticism Schmitt could save to be considered as a "romantic figure".

This is a difficult dilemma to resolve, especially as twentieth-century political thought confronts romantic aesthetics (see Tihanov 2016: 43–58; Roques 2018: 52–74). Moreover, the discussion about Romanticism is paradoxically intertwined, on the one hand, with Schmittian idea of the un-political nature of Romanticism and, on the other, with the idea that Romanticism is able to produce judgments about the political order. The first point is clear: political reflection must engage with German Romanticism since the latter influences indirectly the former. Amidst the dissolution of ultimate grounds, Schmittian "romantic legacy" revolves around the need to establish motives of legal-political order that, even in the absence of a stable ground, remain capable of legitimation.

In this context, irony emerges as a primary element of Romantic aesthetics for constructing this new foundation of legal and political order. On the possibility of establishing a relationship between aesthetic categories and legal categories – such as canon, form, and representation – in Schmittian reflection, especially starting from *Political Romanticism*, a more extensive examination is warranted. This is only one part of a much larger issue concerning the way Schmitt deals with literary and visual arts. The only definition which can capture this connection is that of *Politischer Expressionismus*, according to which Schmittian reflection owes much to the artistic avant-garde and the historical context in which it unfolds (see Kennedy 1988a: 248–249, 1988b)[1]. Following this interpretation, the rationality of Schmitt's legal form – *juridischen Rechtsform* – would be characterized by an irrationality which can be explained only by considering his implicit attachment to the Expressionism. Nevertheless, I am not sure this can be regarded as the main point because Schmitt may not be only the heir of the aesthetic form of Roman Catholicism (see Schmitt 1923) but also the inadvertent theorist of a romantic morphology.

1 The irreducibility of Schmitt to the sphere of law is something that many scholars are prepared to accept (see Noack 1993: 25; Kahn 2003: 69; Mehring 2006: 125–147; Levi 2007: 27–43; Pan 2017: 731–750; Höfele 2022: 10). Some even go so far as to propose a political cubism (see Villinger 1995: 133, 302). In the Italian reception of Schmitt, numerous criticisms have been voiced, focusing mainly on two points: first, the network of references influencing Schmitt's construction of law extends far beyond expressionist art; second, there is often an insistence on Schmitt's Catholicism, which is seen as the reason for his engagement with artists and writers (see Curcio 1930: 480–484; Nicoletti 1990: 65; Nienhaus 1995: 5–48; Garofalo 2020: 39, 61). From this point of view, it is necessary to emphasize that even Catholicism should not be used in a reductionist sense, but rather to stress the importance of Schmitt's relationships with art.

2. Rethinking Romanticism: Irony, Criticism and the Hegelian Context

In his partial reconstruction of Romanticism, Schmitt tries to explain its complex nature, that is, its inherently contradictory character. More precisely, he thinks Romanticism is a phenomenon that is fundamentally alien not only to politics but also to law, because it is based on a particular conception of aesthetics that bears no relation to other fields of knowledge. Indeed, Schmitt states that Romanticism operates in a 'purely aesthetic realm' since 'it pursues an aesthetic effect' and seeks to assign 'a universal role to aesthetics' (Schmitt 2017). Moreover, Romanticism interprets politics according to an 'aesthetic political philosophy' (Schmitt 2017). As a result, Adam Müller's theoretical work (see Müller 1809) should be considered as 'purely aesthetic', especially because the 'core' of all political Romanticism conceives of the State as a 'work of art' (Schmitt 2017). It is in these terms that Schmitt (2017: 125–127) grasps the foundation of Romanticism, namely in the 'claim to extend the aesthetic'. In his confrontation with the Romantic movement, Schmitt deals with the crisis of ultimate ground experienced by German Romanticism and conceives it as a form of aestheticization of politics (see McCormick 1997). In short, Schmitt aims to show there is nothing political in Romanticism, which ends where real political activity begins; in other words, there is 'as little' political Romanticism as there is 'political lyricism' (Schmitt 2017: 162)

Political Romanticism was an immediate success when published. Indeed, György Lukács (see 1928: 695–696) gives it a positive review, and Friedrich Meinecke (see 1920: 292–296) and Ernst Robert Curtius see in it the capacity of 'significantly fulfilling the task that research into Romanticism must undertake' (Bendersky 1988: 465). As mentioned earlier, if Schmitt's point is to give a definition of Romanticism, his problem is to clarify the meaning of the term and its objective referent, as well as to provide a clear reconstruction of it. In pursuit of this goal, Schmitt engages with a vast literature on the connection between Romanticism and the French Revolution (see Burke 1790; Taine 1904; Klemperer 1922), criticizing not only the better-known Adam Müller but also Friedrich Schlegel and Novalis. Moreover, in the central pages, Schmitt reflects on Romantic irony. Schmitt criticizes Novalis for a point which is secondary here, namely the anxiety always generated by aesthetic universe by confusing fiction with reality. For Schmitt (2017: 77), Novalis 'loves only his wife; but with the aid of his imagination he can transform her into thousands of other women'. Schmitt's description of fantasy sounds strikingly similar to Hermann Broch's critique of Romanticism in the first volume of *Die Schlafwandler*, in which the protagonist Pasenow sees in the image of the Madonna the features of the woman he loves (see Broch 1930; Vitzthum 1989: 69–100; Lützeler 2014: 107–126). In any case, Schmitt (2017: 77) writes:

> Art was applied to questions and discussions of political reality "to transform everything into the beloved Sophie and vice versa". This general

> "and vice versa" is the philosopher's stone in the grand alchemy of words that can transform every piece of muck into gold and every piece of gold into muck.

The principle of "and vice versa" is at the core of Romanticism, and precisely for this reason Romanticism should still be rejected by the present politics. But there is a second decisive point for rejecting Romanticism, that is, irony. Here, the figures of Schlegel and Müller become more central. According to Schmitt, even if the originality of Schlegelian thought seems to have been flattened, rather than preserved (see Moretti 1988: 63), both authors conceive irony as unpolitical since it leads from escape to evade from reality, that is, from the "oppression of objectivity" and the resistance that avoids submitting to any limitation. In short, the defense of boundless inner freedom leads Romantics to abandon no possibility.

Here, Schmitt (2017: 72) is very harsh:

> In this way, he preserves his own inner, genial freedom, which consists in not giving up any possibility. By this means, however, he also defends himself against the objection that would necessarily destroy his pretensions: that all the promises and the grandiose projects he has opposed to the limited achievements of others are unmasked as a fraud by his own real production. For him, the concrete accomplishments that are actually at hand amount to nothing more that by products. The protests against having himself or any of his proclamations understood within the limits of current reality. This is not what he is. This is not his ego. At the same time, he is still infinitely many other things and infinitely more than he could ever be in any concrete moment or specific expression. He regards being taken seriously as a violation because he does not want the actual present confused with his infinite freedom.

According to this interpretation, irony places reality at the disposal of the subject; in other words, irony is the means by which the subject is not allowed to make an ultimate decision, which is why the Romantic subject fails to establish anything and why Romanticism represents a crisis of foundation: for Schmitt, foundation takes place, however problematically, through a decision. For this reason, Schmitt (2017: 18) defines Romanticism as 'subjectified occasionalism' – *subjektivierter Occasionalismus*. I do believe both terms coincide with a specific aspect of romantic aesthetics: Novalis' mixing is "subjectivism", whereas Schlegel and Müller's irony is "occasionalism". The fact that the interpretation of German Romanticism as a "subjective dispersion" owes much to the Hegelian perspective can be regarded as the reason why Lukács appreciates it. Although it may be difficult to schematize the relationship between Schmitt and Hegel (see Tronti 1981: 40; Kervégan 1992; Galli 1996: 32–33; Mehring 2013: 305; Preterossi 2022: 75–123), as far as the criticism of Romanticism is concerned, the two seem to agree to each other's interpretation. Indeed, Schmitt (2017: 73) considers Hegel 'who executed romanticism, the state and the world spirit have already become the subjects of the superior irony and intrigue, and they make even the most genial ego into a victim of their Irony'.

At this point, it makes sense to ask whether irony can have anything to do with law (see Frischmann 2014: 156) and, if so, in what sense, whether irony can be understood as an awareness of reality (see Hofmannsthal 1917: 459–461) or an awareness of its contingency (see Rorty 1989). Although Schmitt focuses on the romantic theory of irony which underlies forms of political occasionalism, he highlights two important points. First of all, irony has a complement in romantic theory, namely criticism, which Schmitt, unlike Walter Benjamin, completely fails to address. In fact, criticism coincides with the moment of mediation between the subject and reality, whereas irony represents the "immediate" moment in the attitude to life (see Mann 1918; Moretti 2022: 440–442). Benjamin is one of the most important interpreters of Romanticism of the twentieth century, precisely because, unlike Schmitt, he does not follow Hegelian theory in a naïve way and offers a positive assessment of Romanticism. Moreover, Benjamin does not focus on subjectivism since he sees Romanticism as an epochal movement. This is evident in the centrality given to the theory of literary genres, in particular to the novel as the attempt to shape a historical epoch (see Benjamin 1928: 203–430). Benjamin knows that this alternative is fully faithful to early German Romanticism, as his reflections on Goethe's *Wilhelm Meister* shows. In his views, romantic criticism asserts that only poetry can criticize poetry, and that it is necessary to plunge in the flow of artistic creation to act politically (see W. Benjamin 1920: 7–122, 1924/1925: 123–202; A. Benjamin 2013; Bredekamp 2017: 679–704; Luhr 2002). Secondly, Schmitt does not understand how German Romanticism, in the face of the crisis of foundations, could conceive of irony as the possibility of creating new foundations; on the contrary, in his eyes, irony does not create foundations because it prevents decisions. In short, there is a "proactive aspect" of irony that should not be ignored since it can help to better understand Schmittian theory, in particular the permanent ambiguous relationship he has with Romanticism.

3. Exploring Schmitt's Irony: A Reflection on "Der Spiegel"

Schmitt wrote not only juridical essays but also fiction and satire, texts that are also fundamental to an understanding of his legal theories. Among his most famous works, there are *Schattenrisse* (1913), *Die Buribunken* (1918), and *Die Fackelkraus*, which deals with the figure of Karl Kraus, and it is included in *Bestiarium literaricum* of Franz Blei (see 1920). Much later, Schmitt wrote the lyric *Gesang des Sechzigjährigen* – Song of the Sixty-Year-Old – which illustrates his intention to elaborate a style of writing that goes beyond his legal discourse and accompanies him throughout his life. In 1986, Peter Bürger wrote *Carl Schmitt oder die Fundierung der Politik auf Ästhetik* to argue that Schmittian political theory is based on aesthetics. Even if his thesis is only an intuition not taken up again later, it turns out to be extremely fruitful since Bürger states that the establishment of a legal order based on decision presupposes a hierarchy of values between the "state of exception" and the "state of normality" which can be understood only aesthetically. Thus, Schmitt's theory of the "state of exception" would become clearer by assuming a conception of "legal form" – *juridischen Rechtsform* – that coincides with an aesthetic form, namely a 'dynamic' form capable of integrating life in itself (Bürger 1986: 170–176). Although this aspect is often overlooked, or even openly criticized by scholars, I want to focus on it to clarify the relationship between aesthetics and politics, and therefore also law, so even between political and aesthetic form – *ästhetischen Form des Künstlerischen* (see Landford and Bryan 2016: 208–222; Meierhenrich 2017: 171–216; Meierhenrich and Simons 2017: 3–72), within Schmittian reflection.

Schmitt went on to write another short story, *Der Spiegel* (1912), in which the use of irony and its relationship to law is more explicit than ever. Here, Schmitt talks about Franz Morphenius, a man who is only a soul able to embody different bodies. Recalling the Kafkaesque theme of metamorphosis, his peculiar capacity risks to bring him to dissolution (see Schmitt 1912: 61–62; Grözinger 1992; Kennedy 2004: 43; Mehring 2014: 28). Morphenius is one of the most curious characters created by Schmitt, for example because his name contains the word "form" and refers to Morpheus, namely the Greek god who takes on ever-changing appearances by entering people's dreams and shaping them. Like this god, Schmitt's character is multifaceted, incapable of assuming an ultimate form, therefore condemned to perpetual transformation. Indeed, from his earliest childhood, Franz cannot maintain his convictions, as the narrator ironically describes him:

> I just want to remember that Franz was a good student at high school. In religion class, from 8 to 9 in the morning, he believed in the Trinity (but he could have believed in a quadrinity, quintinity, or sextinity), while in the second hour, the mathematics class, he laughed merrily when the teacher, a bit of a joker, made fun of religion; during history lessons, he burned with patriotism, sometimes crying; and during the reading of Horace, he identified himself as a cosmopolitan kingfisher. Overall, he felt happy; from time to time, he succumbed to bursts of sentimentality, and immediately drew conclusions about his spiritual greatness
>
> (Schmitt 1912: 61–62)

Religious and anticlerical, patriotic, and cosmopolitan, Morphenius seems not to have real identity. In the text, this inclination reaches its climax one afternoon of July when, while resting, his soul transforms itself into a mirror. Franz felt immediately at ease in his new role, which brings him on reflecting the electric trams and milk carts, the delivery boys and the people passing by, in the shop, at lunch, at home in the evening, etc. He, as a mirror, becomes 'unstoppable, friendly and energetic' (Schmitt 1912: 61), allowing him no pause. Moreover, nothing that passes in front of him remains outside because Franz "appropriates everything". In short, through his activity of reflection, he can reproduce the world objectively, to marvel at its plurality and receptivity.

Nevertheless, one day Franz is standing in front of Rosalie Blöing, who is a girl he loved in his childhood, with a suitor. The two turn their backs on him, and he thinks for the first time about the future by asking himself the question: what if the young man were to try to kiss Rosalie? After that, Franz realizes he cannot allow this kiss to happen and must react energetically by avoiding reflecting the kiss to not "disrespect himself". Even if he makes a great effort by trying to scream, his excitement prevents him from moving, and leads him proceeding in the only way a mirror can behave, that is, by breaking itself. However, by a twist of fate, Rosalie's clumsy suitor leans his elbow against the mirror at that moment, and so when Franz falls into pieces, no one is surprised, and no one notices it is not only an external destruction but rather an "internal" one.

According to Schmitt, "rationalists" can be satisfied by such an explanation, and he concludes the story by asking: 'What does a rationalist know about real life?' (Schmitt 1912: 62). In terms that will be explored further, Schmitt's story alludes to the value of fiction (see Villinger 1992: 191–222). Moreover, Morphenius reminds us of the theses of Schmitt's youthful satires, and Schmitt seems to have sympathy for him since Franz tries to react. The thesis of his story seems to be that aesthetic fiction cannot be reduced to an objective reflection of the "real" world (see Türk 2008: 73–89) because it would be ineffective, but above all because it cannot "disrespect itself". For Schmitt, fiction is always action, even if we have not the proper means to perceive it. In this sense, the narrator's conviction at the beginning is particularly intriguing: 'I am convinced', he states explicitly, 'that there is absolutely nothing dead, that there are no dead things'. He continues: 'I think it is undeniable that even the flowerpot, the tree trunk and the doily are living beings, individualities and, why not, even human beings'. The question is merely terminological, and indeed the narrator concludes by asking: 'If there are human beings that can seriously be defined as tree trunks or doilies, why shouldn't there be tree trunks and doilies that are human beings?' (Schmitt 1912: 61).

This statement can be understood, in an almost literal sense, as the failure to free oneself from the mythical realism of antiquity, as well as the possibility of admitting an active practice of the material world and its constant exchange with the human, that is, the space of metamorphosis. The fact that Franz does not simply enter into a mirror, but rather becomes a mirror, suggests Schmittian attempt to criticize the idea of aesthetics as mere reflection because it risks producing a confused mixing of fiction and reality. The story illustrates the limits of a certain interpretation of aesthetics, which is challenged by the Schmittian proposal of an active aesthetics that can also involve law and politics. Morphenius is clearly a victim of the first idea of aesthetics until he decides not to identify with Rosalie's suitor. The question remains whether the story could have had a simpler solution, such as the transformation of Morphenius into the suitor. Instead of denying his identity, he affirms it, and this coincides with the first time he does not merely reflect something. He does not remain passive, and that is enough to make him a positive figure in Schmitt's eyes.

I think *The Mirror* could be considered as an excellent example of the role played by romantic aesthetics in Schmittian thought because it is an actual activity that manifests itself both as rejection of mere, by not reflecting the image of the suitor, and as attempt to imagine an alternative form, even though it is destined to be broken. In this sense, I propose describing Schmitt as an "ironic thinker" by embracing an interpretation that fully appreciates the necessity of narrative, the need for storytelling in the broadest sense, and the implicit acceptance of its political significance facilitated by the mediation of a not overly veiled irony. This detail allows me to refer to what I wrote above on Schmittian conflictual relationship with Romanticism, as well as to state they cannot be considered as fragmented identity narratives since they can find their rightful place and value within a well-articulated comprehensive view. In literary terms, even if the mirror is now shattered, it may not be necessary to abandon it altogether.

4. Foundational Challenges: Revisiting Carl Schmitt in Post-Foundational Political Thought

Schmitt's irony in its inherent connection to politics and law, together with Schmitt's ambiguous relationship to Romanticism and aesthetics, is a good starting point for re-reading Schmitt in the contemporary debate on post-foundationalism. As Oliver Marchart elucidates, post-foundational political thought grounds itself in the examination of the distinction between "politics" and "the political" (*die Politik* and *das Politische*) introduced by Schmitt in the preface to the Italian edition of *Le categorie del "politico"* (see Schmitt 1971). Marchart's thesis revolves around this fascinating discrepancy or, better, this peculiar and unconventional division. Like Chantal Mouffe and Ernesto Laclau, Marchart interprets Schmittian work through *The Concept of the Political.* Furthermore, Marchart links Schmitt to Martin Heidegger by highlighting their common political positions and interpreting Schmitt as the one who most radically initiated the crisis of foundationalism within twentieth-century political theory (see Mouffe 1999: 1–6; Laclau 2007; Marchart 2007), as was already the case in the Italian debate on the autonomy of the political (see Tronti 1972: 285–312, 1998: 549–562). According to this perspective, the legal-political order cannot be founded on truth, since *auctoritas non veritas facit legem* – authority, not truth, creates law (see Žižek 1999: 18–37). Thus, paradoxically, post-foundationalism meets Schmitt's opposition to foundationalism, although Schmitt's importance in Marchart's work is limited to deconstruction. The first alternative thus has a purely deconstructive aim.

Similarly, the second alternative reads a crisis of ultimate ground in Schmitt's thought from the perspective of political theology (see Schmittian references such as Grossheutschi 1996; Galli 1996; Marder 2010; Kervégan 2011; Vatter 2021; and the contributions to the Italian collection edited by Duso 1981). Rather than emphasizing deconstruction, as Marchart does, they speak of the nihilism inherent in Schmittian thought and associate it with Nietzsche. More precisely, the focus shifts to the significance of political theology, which scholars conceive, rather than as grounding of politics in theology, as the radical insistence on a foundation entrusted to the *Entscheidung*, that is, the decision of sovereignty. As a result, Schmittian position is seen characterized by a longing for a stable ground in the midst of its absence, in the sense that it hovers over a void. To sum up, from this contribution emerges several questions, like that of the right place where to put Schmittian thought, namely next to Heidegger or Nietzsche, and what kind of implication this positioning can have.

I do believe there is a third way to consider, that is, the interpretation of Lukács, Ball, and Löwith, which considers Schmitt as a romantic figure. This third interpretation suggests that, likewise the romantics, Schmitt is faced with a crisis and a questioning of traditional foundations, even if he seeks to give an answer to this dissolution. In this way, his position can be understood as the fascination that Dionysus of Euripides exerted on the German world (see Frank 1982; Nienhaus 1995: 22). Rooted in early Romanticism, this view sees in Dionysus both the rationalist destruction of the old religious faith (signaled by the end of the cult of traditional deities in Euripides) and the potential of a new religiosity that believes in a new god emerging from the East. Dionysus, namely the god reborn before birth, represents a "new god", a "god of the future", so a deity to come. Thus, Dionysus embodies both the rational destruction of faith and the overcoming of the crisis of meaning caused by rationalism.

This ambiguity is at the core of Romanticism, and the authors of the twentieth century are very interested in it. The so-called "conservative revolution" interprets it as the possibility of a "third realm" (see Moller van den Bruck 1923; Lauryssens 2003), whereas Schmitt sees something closer to the early Jena Romanticism since he recognizes the irreparable loss of a transcendent foundation and, at the same time, the need to find a solution to this absence. Evidently, this issue deserves further studies and elaborations, especially regarding the Schmittian conception of "law" (*Recht*). As I try to illustrate, this conception differs from a political theology often associated with Thomas Hobbes, despite the frequent references to Hobbes in the secondary literature on Schmitt. Indeed, Hobbes advocates a symbolic politics (see Creuzer 1819), whereas Schmitt embodies an ironic attitude, even by recognizing the impossibility of maintaining the stability of Hobbesian "political theology". In this regard, irony underlies Schmittian critique of "occasionalism" within the Romanticism, even if Schmitt himself is a deeply ironic writer (see Preterossi 2022: 120–135). According to the crucial role of irony for understanding both aesthetics and political theory, I do believe in the importance to explore more deeply the relationship between irony and law, rooted in German Romanticism, in Schmittian reflections. In fact, irony is a form of narrative that, even if lacking a traditional metaphysical foundation, can be conceived as something "foundational". If one takes seriously the role of irony in Carl Schmitt's thought, the focus should not only be on the foundation as fiction, as in deconstructive readings of Schmitt, but rather on the idea that fiction itself can constitute a new foundation: if the aesthetic principle does not reproduce the real but produces it, it also establishes it. Although the ironic element moves away from strong metaphysical claims, irony retains a legitimizing foundation for the literary or the political horizon. In short, irony can be interpreted as acting as a bridge between legitimacy and foundation.

Bibliography

Ball, H. (1924) 'Carl Schmitts politische Theologie', *Hochland*, 2, pp. 261–286.

Bendersky, J.W. (1988) 'Politische Romantik: Intellectual Critique and Enduring Scholarly Influence', in Quaritsch, H. (ed.), *Complexio Oppositorum: Über Carl Schmitt*, Berlin: Duncker & Humblot, pp. 462–490.

Benjamin, A. (2013) *Working with Walter Benjamin: Recovering a Political Philosophy*, Edinburgh: Edinburgh University Press.

Benjamin, W. (1920) 'Der Begriff der Kunstkritik in der deutschen Romantik', in Schweppenhäuser, H., and Tiedemann, R. (eds.), *Gesammelte Schriften I.1*, Frankfurt am Main: Suhrkamp, pp. 7–122.

Benjamin, W. (1924) 'Goethes Wahlverwandtschaften', in Schweppenhäuser, H., and Tiedemann, R. (eds.), *Gesammelte Schriften I.1*, Frankfurt am Main: Suhrkamp, 1925, pp. 123–202.

Benjamin, W. (1928) 'Ursprung des deutschen Trauerspiels', in Schweppenhäuser, H., and Tiedemann, R. (eds.), *Gesammelte Schriften I.1*, Frankfurt am Main: Suhrkamp, pp. 203–430.

Bredekamp, H. (2017) 'Walter Benjamin's Esteem for Carl Schmitt', in Meierhenrich, J., and Simons, O. (eds.), *The Oxford Handbook of Carl Schmitt*, New York: Oxford University Press, pp. 679–704.

Broch, H. (1930) *Die Schlaffwandler*, Frankfurt am Main: Suhrkamp Verlag.

Bürger, P. (1986) 'Carl Schmitt oder die Fundierung der Politik auf Ästhetik', in Bürger, C. (ed.), *Zerstörung, Rettung Des Mythos Durch Licht*, Frankfurt am Main: Suhrkamp, pp. 170–176.

Burke, E. (1790) *Reflections on the Revolution in France*, London: J. Dodsley.

Creuzer, F. (1819) *Symbolik und Mythologie der alten Völker I: Allgemeine Beschreibung des symbolischen und mytischen Kreises*, Leipzig: Darmstadt.

Curcio, C. (1930) 'Tendenze nuove della dottrina tedesca: C. Schmitt', *Lo Stato*, 4, pp. 480–484.

Duso, G. (ed.) (1981) *La politica oltre lo Stato: Carl Schmitt*, Venezia: Arsenale cooperativa editrice.

Frank, M. (1982) *Der kommende Gott*, Frankfurt a.M.: Suhrkamp.

Frischmann, B. (ed.) (2014) *Ironie in Philosophie, Literatur und Recht*, Würzburg: Königshausen & Neumann.

Galli, C. (1996) *Genealogia della politica: Carl Schmitt e la crisi del pensiero politico moderno*, Bologna: Il Mulino.

Garofalo, L. (2020) *Intrecci schmittiani*, Bologna: Il Mulino.

Grossheutschi, F. (1996) *Carl Schmitt und die Lehre vom Katechon*, Berlin: Duncker & Humblot.

Grözinger, K. (1992) *Kafka und die Kabbala*, Frankfurt am Main: Eichborn.

Höfele, A. (2022) *Carl Schmitt und die Literatur*, Berlin: Duncker & Humblot.

Hofmannsthal, H.V. (1917) 'Preuße und Österreicher: Ein Schema', in Schoeller, B.V. (ed.), *Gesammelte Werke in zehn Einzelbänden. Reden und Aufsätze II (1914–1924)*, Frankfurt am Main: Fischer Taschenbuch Verlag, 1979, pp. 459–461.

Kahn, V. (2003) 'Hamlet or Hecuba: Carl Schmitt's Decision', *Representations*, 83, pp. 67–96.

Kennedy, E. (1988a) 'A Politischer Expressionismus: Die kulturkritischen und metaphysischen Ursprünge des Begriffs des Politischen von Carl Schmitt', in Quaritsch, H. (ed.), *Complexio Oppositorum: Über Carl Schmitt*, Berlin: Duncker & Humblot, pp. 233–253.

Kennedy, E. (1988b) 'Carl Schmitt und Hugo Ball: Ein Beitrag zum Thema *politischer Expressionismus*', *Zeitschrift für Politik*, 35, pp. 143–162.

Kennedy, E. (2004) *Constitutional Failure: Carl Schmitt in Weimar*, Durham: Duke University Press.

Kervégan, J.-F. (1992) *Hegel, Carl Schmitt: Le politique entre speculation et positivité*, Paris: PUF.

Kervégan, J.-F. (2011) *Que faire de Carl Schmitt?* Paris: Gallimard.

Klemperer, V. (1922) 'Romantik und französische Romantik', in Prang, H. (ed.), *Begriffsbestimmung der Romantik*, Darmstadt: Wissenschaftliche Buchgesellschaft, 1968.

Laclau, E. (2007) *On Populist Reason*, London: Verso.

Langford, P., and Bryan, I. (2016) 'Beyond the Jurist as a Theologian of Legal Science: The Question of Carl Schmitt and the International Legal Order', in Arvidsson, M., Brännström, L., and Minkkinen, P. (eds.), *The Contemporary Relevance of Carl Schmitt Law, Politics, Theology*, New York: Routledge, pp. 208–222.

Lauryssens, S. (2003) *The Man Who Invented the Third Reich: The Life and Times of Arthur Möller Van Den Bruck*, New York: Sutton Publishing.

Levi, N. (2007) 'Carl Schmitt and the Question of the Aesthetic', *New German Critique*, pp. 27–43.

Löwith, K. (1935) 'Der okkasionelle Dezisionismus von C. Schmitt', in *Gesammelte Abhandlungen: Zur Kritik der geschichtlichen Existenz*, Stuttgart: Kohlhammer, 1960, pp. 93–126.

Luhr, G. (2002) *Ästhetische Kritik der Moderne: Über das Verhältnis Walter Benjamins und der jüdischen Intelligenz zu Stefan George*, Marburg: LiteraturWissenschaft.

Lukács, G. (1928) 'Carl Schmitt: Politische Romantik', in *Frühschriften II: Geschichte und Klassenbewusstsein*, Luchterhand: Darmstadt und Neuwied, 1977, pp. 695–696.

Lukács, G. (1954) *Die Zerstörung der Vernunft*, Neuwied and Berlin: Luchterhand.

Lützeler, P.M. (2014) 'Hermann Brochs "Pasenow oder die Romantik" und Carl Schmitts "Politische Romantik"', in Wohlleben, D., and Lützeler, P.M. (eds.), *Hermann Broch und die Romantik*, Berlin and Boston: De Gruyter, pp. 107–126.

Mann, T. (1918) *Betrachtungen eines Unpolitischen*, Berlin: Fischer, 2009.

Marchart, O. (2007) *Post-Foundational Political Thought*, Edinburgh: Edinburgh University Press.

Marder, M. (2010) *Groundless Existence: The Political Ontology of Carl Schmitt*, New York: Continuum.

McCormick, J.P. (1997) *Carl Schmitt's Critique of Liberalism: Against Politics as Technology*, Cambridge: Cambridge University Press.

Mehring, R. (2006) 'Übertdung des Ästhetizismus? Carl Schmitts selbstinquisitorische Romantikkritik', *Athenäum*, 16, pp. 125–147.

Mehring, R. (2013) 'Carl Schmitt und Hegel: Romantikkritik und bürgerliche Verfassung', *Hegel-Jahrbuch*, 19, pp. 304–311.

Mehring, R. (2014) *Carl Schmitt: A Biography*, Cambridge: Polity Press.

Meierhenrich, J. (2017) 'Fearing the Disorder of Things', in Meierhenrich, J., and Simons, O. (eds.), *The Oxford Handbook of Carl Schmitt*, New York: Oxford University Press, pp. 171–216.

Meierhenrich, J., and Simons, O. (2017) 'A Fanatic of Order in an Epoch of Confusing Turmoil: The Political, Legal, and Cultural Thought of Carl Schmitt', in Meierhenrich, J., and Simons, O. (eds.), *The Oxford Handbook of Carl Schmitt*, New York: Oxford University Press, pp. 3–72.

Meinecke, F. (1920) 'Politische Romantik: Von Dr. Carl Schmitt-Dorotic', *Historische Zeitschrift*, pp. 292–296.

Moeller van den Bruck, A. (1923) *Das dritte Reich*, Hamburg and Wandsbek: Hanseatische Verlagsanstalt.

Moretti, G. (1988) *Hestia: Interpretazione del romanticismo tedesco*, Roma: Ianua.

Moretti, G. (2022) 'Friedrich Nietzsche tra Martin Heidegger e Thomas Mann', *Comparatismi*, 7, pp. 438–443.

Mouffe, C. (1999) 'Introduction: The Schmitt Challenge', in Mouffe, C. (ed.), *The Challenge of Carl Schmitt*, London and New York: Verso, pp. 1–6.

Müller, A.H. (1809) *Die Elemente der Staatskunst*, Berlin: Sander.

Nicoletti, M. (1990) *Trascendenza e Potere: La teologia politica di Carl Schmitt*, Brescia: Morcelliana.

Nienhaus, S. (1995) 'Carl Schmitt fra poeti e letterati', in Schmitt, C. (ed.), *Aurora Boreale: Tre studi sugli elementi, lo spirito e l'attualità dell'opera di Theodor Daübler*, Napoli: Edizioni Scientifiche Italiane, pp. 5–48.

Noack, P. (1993) *Carl Schmitt: Eine Biographie*, München: Propyläen.

Pan, D. (2017) 'Tragedy as Exception in Carl Schmitt's *Hamlet or Hecuba*', in Meierhenrich, J., and Simons, O. (eds.), *The Oxford Handbook of Carl Schmitt*, New York: Oxford University Press, pp. 731–750.

Preterossi, G. (2022) *Teologia politica e diritto*, Bari-Roma: Laterza.

Roques, C.E. (2018) 'Bridging the Political Gaps: The Interdiscursive Qualities of Political Romanticism in the Weimar Republic', *Contributions to the History of Concepts*, 13, pp. 52–74.

Rorty, R. (1989) *Kontingenz, Ironie und Solidarität*, Frankfurt am Main: Suhrkamp.

Schmitt, C. (1912) 'Der Spiegel', *Die Rheinlande*, 22, pp. 61–62.

Schmitt, C. (1918) 'Die Buribunken. Ein geschichtsphilosophischer Versuch', *Summa*, 4, pp. 89–106.

Schmitt, C. (1920) 'Die Fackelkraus', in Blei, F. (ed.), *Bestiarium Literaricum*, München: Georg Müller, pp. 64–66; in *Das große Bestiarium Literatur*, Hamburg: Europäische Verlagsanstalt, 1995, pp. 57–59.

Schmitt, C. (1922) *Politische Theologie: Vier Kapitel zur Lehre von der Souveränität*, München and Leipzig: Duncker & Humblot.

Schmitt, C. (1923) *Römischer Katholizismus und politische Form*, Stuttgart: Klett-Cotta.

Schmitt, C. (1927) 'Der Begriff des Politischen', *Archiv für Sozialwissenschaft und Sozialpolitik*, 58, pp. 1–33.

Schmitt, C. (1919) *Political Romanticism*, London and New York: Routledge, 2017.

Schmitt, C. (1971) *Premessa all'edizione italiana*, in Schmitt, C., *Le categorie del "politico"*, Bologna, Il Mulino, pp. 21–26.

Schmitt, C., and Eisler, F. (1913) *Schattenrisse*, Berlin: Skiamacheten Verlag; in Villinger, I. (ed.), *Carl Schmitts Kulturkitik der Moderne*, Berlin: Akademie Verlag, 1995, pp. 11–67.

Sombart, N. (1991) *Die deutschen Männer und ihre Feinde: Carl Schmitt – ein deutsches Schicksal zwischen Männerbund und Matriarchatsmythos*, Frankfurt am Main: Fischer Taschenbuch.

Taine, H. (1904) 'La Révolution, la conquête jacobine', in *Les Origines de la France contemporaine II*, Paris: Hachette.

Tihanov, G. (2016) 'The Post-Romantic Syndrome: Reflections on Work, Wealth, and Trade from Adam Müller to Ernst Jünger', *Primerjalna književnost*, 39, pp. 43–58.

Tronti, M. (1972) 'Sull'autonomia del politico', in *Il demone della politica: Antologia di scritti (1958–2015)*, Bologna: Il Mulino, 2017, pp. 285–312.

Tronti, M. (1981) 'Marx e Schmitt: un problema storico-teorico', in Duso, G. (ed.), *La politica oltre lo Stato: Carl Schmitt*, Venezia: Arsenale cooperativa editrice, pp. 25–40.

Tronti, M. (1998) 'Karl und Carl', in *Il demone della politica: Antologia di scritti (1958–2015)*, Bologna: Il Mulino, 2017, pp. 549–562.

Türk, J. (2008) 'The Intrusion: Carl Schmitt's Non-Mimetic Logic of Art', *Telos*, 142, pp. 73–89.

Vatter, M. (2021) *Divine Democracy: Political Theology after Carl Schmitt*, Oxford: Oxford University Press.

Villinger, I. (1992) 'Politische Fiktionen: Carl Schmitts literarische Experimente', in Dotzler, B.J. (ed.), *Technopathologien*, Leiden: Brill, pp. 191–222.

Villinger, I. (ed.) (1995) *Carl Schmitts Kulturkritik der Moderne: Text, Kommentar Analyse der "Schattenrisse" des Johannes Negelinus*, Berlin: Akademie Verlag.

Vitzthum, W.G. (1989) 'Hermann Broch und Carl Schmitt', in Heideking, J., Hufnagel, G., and Knipping, F. (eds.), *Wege der Zeitgeschichte. Festschrift zum 65: Geburtstag von Gerhard Schulz*, Berlin and New York: De Gruyter, pp. 69–100.

Žižek, S. (1999) 'Carl Schmitt in the Age of Post-Politics', in Mouffe, C. (ed.), *The Challenge of Carl Schmitt*, London and New York: Verso, pp. 18–37.

4 Public Choice and Post-Foundationalism

Constitutions, Democracy and Economic Rationality

Giacomo Brioni

1. Introduction

In the course of this paper, I will undertake a comparison between public choice theory and post-foundationalism. Public choice is the line of inquiry that applies the main tenets of economic theory to the study of politics and law (voting rules, coalition forming, the relationship between institutions and individual behavior, etc.). The way for this discipline was paved in the second half of the twentieth century by the studies of prominent economists, such as Kenneth Arrow, Duncan Black, Anthony Downs, James Buchanan and Gordon Tullock, William Riker, and Mancur Olson, among others[1].

Although at first glance the economic approach seems wholly foreign to post-foundationalism in terms of philosophical language and political outlook, I will show that they can be made consistent, at least as far as the methodological assumptions are concerned. This common ground will serve as a starting point for a reciprocal critique. I will first point out that a post-foundationalist reading of public choice can help to highlight the conceptual difficulties of its contractarian strand (constitutional political economy). Then, I will proceed to show that the same criticism applies to the ultra-political paradigm of radical democracy that is embraced by some post-foundationalist thinkers. Taken together, my arguments will amount to a non-contractarian defense of procedural rationality.

2. Methodological Remarks on the Economic Approach to Political Theory

Though the discussion about the crisis of foundationalism in political philosophy is multifaceted and involves many authors with different positions, some

1 For practical reasons I will adopt a more inclusive, if less precise, definition of public choice, which essentialy equates it with the economic approach. That is, I will not restrict it to Buchanan and Tullock's contributions, nor will I make any distinctions between public choice and social choice theory, and so forth.

DOI: 10.4324/9781003471066-5

common threads can be identified. The first and most important consists in recognizing the autonomy of the political (for this reason, I will sometimes refer to post-foundationalism as the "autonomistic thesis"). This means, as Schmitt (2007: 23–27) famously highlighted, that the political is marked by its own inner distinctions (to Schmitt, the friend/enemy one) that cannot be reduced to those defining other realms of human coexistence (e.g., the aesthetic, moral, economic, or social). Furthermore, the political is assigned ontological priority over every other form of activity. Oliver Marchart has condensed these features in a 'triple thesis with respect to the autonomization of politics', whereby 'politics is now posed . . . as specific (by being different from other spheres), autonomous (which means independent and autarchic), and as a "first cause", that is to say, as being prior to anything social' (Marchart 2007: 49). All of this ultimately leads to what in contemporary left-Heideggerian terms is called "the political difference" (modeled after Martin Heidegger's ontological difference): the idea that politics (*die Politik, la politique*), that is, the ordinary life of institutions and legal procedures, is always conditional on the political (*das Politische*, *le politique*) as an unruly moment of grounding and ungrounding (e.g. Marchart 2007: 18–25, 36)[2].

To someone operating in this framework, a philosophy of politics based on economic reasoning and which draws on the related conceptual toolboxes of decision theory and game theory must appear as a *bête noire*. This kind of approach seems to embody the core structure of the foundationalist reasoning, in that 'it first provides a set of principles (the economic "laws") which are presented as the essence of politics (what politics is "really" about), and, secondly, it locates the ground (the economic "base") outside of, or beyond,

2 Marchart's contribution will be quoted frequently as the chief representative of the post-foundational paradigm, mainly because it was the first attempt to give a coherent synthesis of the latter. The reader should however be aware that it is by no means the only theoretical option. In a more recent book that is comparable to Marchart's for the breadth of its philosophical intention, Esposito (see 2020: xxi–xxii) has noticed that the selection of authors Marchart makes and the commonalities he stresses between them are dependent on his post-heideggerian ontological option. Esposito, for instance, divorces Claude Lefort from Heidegger's legacy by attributing to the latter a quasi-nihilistic attitude because of the emphasis on the "negative" moment, on the "unpolitical" foundation of politics. On the other hand, Lefort is credited with the idea of an "instituent paradigm" which points to the entanglement between the political and the social spheres. Throughout the present paper, I will focus as far as possible on giving operative descriptions of the concepts in play, in order to apply them to the field of explanatory political theory as a common ground of comparison between post-foundationalism and the economic approach. This means that I will forego some accuracy in outlining the differences between individual philosophical stances, unless they have some direct bearing on the development of the argument. In the case just quoted, for instance, the problem seems to be one of attribution more than of strict theoretical disagreement. Both Marchart and Esposito identify the post-foundational stance with the idea of the non-trascendent autonomy of the political and of groundless or conflictualist democracy in the neo-machiavellian fashion. However, Marchart forces this features in the post-Heideggerian scheme while Esposito does not do so.

the immediate realm of politics, the latter being turned into a merely super-structural affair' (Marchart 2007: 12). Along with sociology, economics is held responsible for having deprived political theory of its specific subject matter, thus reproducing on the academic level the logic of depoliticization warned against by Schmitt (see Marchart 2007: 51–52. One can find similar indictments coming from positions that claim substantive normative content for political philosophy; see Barry 1965).

In this section I aim to show that the economic approach, if correctly represented, can be regarded as non-foundationalist, and that its features make it a viable alternative when compared to the autonomistic thesis in the explanatory territory. I will employ as a tool the famous classification of types of explanatory political theory put forward by Robert Nozick at the beginning of *Anarchy, State, and Utopia*. Nozick (2013: 6) writes that

> the possible ways of understanding the political realm are as follows: (1) to fully explain it in terms of the nonpolitical; (2) to view it as emerging from the nonpolitical but irreducible to it, a mode of organization of nonpolitical factors understandable only in terms of novel political principles; or (3) to view it as a completely autonomous realm.

Proponents of the autonomy of the political are opposed to option (1) – what Nozick aptly calls 'fundamental explanations' (Nozick 2013: 6) – and seem to fall squarely into category (3). I formulate this statement with a degree of caution, because a theory like Schmitt's could also be made to fit model (2). This is due to the fact that Schmitt describes the political less in terms of a domain than as a criterion that can be used to measure any kind of tension between human collectives: 'The political is the most extreme antagonism, and every concrete antagonism becomes that much more political the closer it approaches the most extreme point, that of the friend-enemy grouping' (Schmitt 2007: 29). In other words, Schmitt's model could be interpreted as a kind of mixed emergentism: the political in its pure form is a qualitatively distinct mode of being, but it can be traced in the process of its appearance by looking at the degree of conflict in nonpolitical situations. Moreover, as we observe the articulation of the autonomistic position, we can distinguish another element of theoretical hierarchy, that is, the priority of the political over politics. The plane which can be properly understood as a fully constituted domain derives from something which shares with it some features, but is almost irreconcilable in terms of intensity. Therefore, we could describe this passage as a second process of emergence – although, in post-foundational terms, it looks more like a neutralization, a sort of negative emergence that covers up the tensions lurking underneath it (see Schmitt 2007: 30). I have taken up the language of emergentism to illustrate the post-foundationalist methodology because there seems to be an increasing tendency in the literature to move away from the "decisionistic" stance, as it is taken to still retain some foundationalist echoes, and to embrace a more "processualistic" description of politics. This is evident, for instance, in Esposito's (2020: 168) exposition of a paradigm of political ontology based on the concept of 'instituent praxis', which supplements the Schmittian insight with the French-Machiavellian route of Claude Lefort and the juridical institutionalism of Maurice Hauriou and Santi Romano. Esposito still emphasizes the pivotal role of political conflict as embodying the moment of division which lies at the heart of society, but he places it in the continuous and immanent dimension of historical experience, wherein every act of social change is always a '*creatio ex aliquo*' (Esposito 2020: 169).

Let's turn to the economic approach. If one understands it as Marchart does in the passage quoted earlier, the most intuitive identification is with paradigm (1). However, this is only the effect of a superficial reading, and option (2) seems again to be the most appropriate one. In line with the contemporary self-understanding of the discipline, the essence of economics does not lie in the study of, let's say, how wealth is generated, how the market works, and so on. As the well-known definition proposed by Lionel Robbins (1984: 16) states, economics is 'the science which studies human behavior as a relationship between ends and scarce means which have alternative uses'. In other words, economic analysis isn't directed at examining any specific or closed set of human relations – for example, the productive relations that ground the structure-superstructure dichotomy in Marxist theory (see Buchanan and Tullock 1999: 12–13). It rather aims at building a logic of choice whose only external determination is the fact of scarcity. This framework can also be extended beyond the means-ends scheme that is at the center of Robbins' definition, in order to include the study of the selection of ends *via* the concept of opportunity cost (compare Harsanyi 1976: 93 to Buchanan 1999).

The outcome is a philosophy of human action (as pictured in Mises 1998) applicable to different modes of interaction – namely, the economic and the political – neither of which necessarily grounds the other, but all of which can be seen to emerge from the same formal structure. This is not to deny that, in some instances, concepts belonging to the market sphere such as exchange, equilibrium, and so forth may have been employed too directly for political theorizing, in a way resembling standard foundational procedure (consider as an example Bruno Leoni's debate with Duncan Black as reported in Masala 2003: 151 ff.; see also Buchanan and Tullock 1999: 16–24). However, this can be attributed to the influence of normative preferences in specific models, more than to an orientation inherent in the theory itself. The economic approach, in the end, shares with the post-foundational perspective the ambition of generality in explanation. Both can be understood as being criterion-oriented more than domain-oriented; the former, however, seeks to be more exhaustive, because it refuses to treat the political as a black box and aims to analyze its praxeological elements.

The economic approach is further qualified by the way it models human agency, building on three theoretical pillars: methodological individualism and the behavioral assumptions of self-interest and utility maximization. Although post-foundationalism seems more inclined to take a collectivist stance in defining the basic social entities, all of these principles are in tune with the background political realism of the autonomistic thesis. Both paradigms aim to articulate the basic premise of the heterogeneity of human ends. The economic theory of politics tackles this point by stating that no social ideal exists apart from the constraints of localized instrumental action. Any objective is advanced in the world as a part of an individual preference ranking, and as a claim to a bundle of scarce resources (see Leoni 2004). A study of collective action, therefore, must start from the analysis of how the multiple claims which constitute society interact with each other (or, in public choice terms, from the analysis of reciprocal externalities, see Buchanan and Tullock 1999: 43 62). Accordingly, institutions are not seen as transcendent sets of ends to be imposed on society, but as constraints which embody alternative incentive structures for individual behavior (see Brennan and Buchanan 2000): the politico-legal order, in an ontological sense, is always a matter of sectional good (see Olson 1965) and an endogenous structure. This is especially relevant for the question of how democracy is to be conceptualized, that is, both the main field of application claimed by the autonomistic thesis and the first subject for which the economic approach was elaborated (see Downs 1957). If we look at its systematic critique of collective concepts, as well as to its processualistic opening, the economic approach stands at the polar opposite of foundationalist theories.

The post-foundational theorist could, however, call into question the restrictiveness of the assumptions of the economic approach, by saying that it unduly generalizes a structure of behavior which is anchored to the specific institutions of the market (see Barry 1965: 282). Here we have to be clear about the methodological trade-offs with which every theory is faced. Let's identify three of the main desirable features of a theory: (1) economy (the ability to explain a lot with few assumptions), (2) predictive power, and (3) descriptive realism. It is difficult for any given proposition to maximize all of these characteristics, the most sensible trade-offs being between (1) and (3) or between (2) and (3). Historically, the economic approach has been seen to fit fairly well (1) and (2), as various authors have emphasized (e.g., Friedman 1953; Becker 1976; Harsanyi 1976). Some strands of the theory have sought to enchance (3) by studying instances of cooperative behavior that seem to defy the self-interest assumption (e.g., Ostrom 1990). However, these attempts often end up superimposing the action of cultural norms or alternative incentive structures on preference formation, rather than directly questioning the behavioral postulates. Moreover, if one tries to broaden too much the scope of the chosen assumptions, the theory risks losing definition and is liable to become a series of empty descriptive propositions or a tautological exercise (see Barry 1978: 33). While evaluating a theory, one should also be aware of the set of problems it is applied to. If we think about contemporary representative democracy, for instance, one can see that strategic behavior can be generalized effectively even if it isn't exhaustive of all the possibilities of interaction, simply because in the competition of groups it pays off to enact a maximizing strategy, to the point that this feature crowds out the others (compare Riker 1962; Friedman 1953: 21–22; Buchanan and Tullock 1999: 21–22).

3. The Constitutional Perspective

In the previous section I have shown that the methodology of public choice can be interpreted through a post-foundational lens. However, we must not forget that a sizeable chunk of public choice theorizing has been taken up by the grand project of constitutional political economy, mainly developed by James M. Buchanan and other scholars belonging to the Virginia School. Constitutional political economy is an essentially normative enterprise, which strives to show how a population of rational egoists could agree on the common economic advantage of adopting institutions resembling those of constitutional democracy. Along with John Rawls, David Gauthier, and others, Buchanan has taken part in the renaissance of the contractarian argument in the last century (on which see Weale 2020). This is problematic, because contractarianism can be identified as the cornerstone of modern political rationalism, with its abstract individualistic framework and the stress on people's ability to consciously design and control their institutions, and to reach agreement on background principles by way of impartial reflection. Before turning to the critical comments, I will present the main lines of Buchanan's theory of constitutions in the rest of the current section. The exposition will revolve around the three main functions public choice ascribes to constitutional design: (1) to put in place a framework that facilitates transactions; (2) to canalize long-term uncertainty through procedural rules; (3) to diffuse and control power in society.

Function (1) is highlighted by the economic interpretation of Hobbesian anarchy (see Buchanan 2000; Brennan and Buchanan 2000). The basic features of the social order (property rights, contracts, and promises) have the incentive structure of a public good. Individuals recognize that cooperation yields better collective outcomes and may even agree with each other that this is so. However, regardless of the possibility for communication between players, there is a strong unilateral incentive to defect from agreements, because agents see that higher short-term payoffs can be gained from such a move. In the standard prisoner's dilemma situation, defection is the dominant strategy, leading to a sub-optimal equilibrium: irrespective of what the other player does, it is always better to act in this way, either to secure positive gains or to avoid complete dispossession. This is Hobbes' *bellum*, where order is non-existent (or a rare and unstable event), and mutual untrust and expoliation are the standard practice.

The main problem of this arrangement, from the standpoint of the present analysis, is the high correlation between transaction costs and strategic behavior. Agreements – especially in the shape of 'half-spot, half-forward' (or entirely forward) contracts (De Jasay 1989: 23) – are the instruments that allow people to project themselves forward through time. In economic terms, the determinants of growth – division of labor due to comparative advantage, capital accumulation, saving, investment, technological innovation – are conditional on the existence of stable institutions with credible third-party enforcement mechanisms. The point here is not only that in their absence people would not be able to reach Pareto-optimal positions; rather, it is that they would actively engage in forms of resource-wasteful behavior represented by the 'predation-defense effort' of the Hobbesian state of nature (Buchanan 2000: 37). Without a framework of collective action that makes human interaction predictable, little opportunities exist to capture gains from trade, especially in *n*-people groups where the incentive for defection is directly proportional to the increasing difficulty to detect individual non-cooperators (see Buchanan 2000: 86). The definition of property rights and the setting up of an external enforcer – the 'protective state' (Buchanan 2000: 88 ff.) – is what Buchanan (2000: 41) identifies as the first stage of the 'constitutional contract'. One noteworthy feature of this model (which will be fully employed later in my discussion) is that the transition from the starting 'natural distribution' (Buchanan 2000: 75) of resources to a set of rights properly understood may already require political bargaining and redistribution to generate agreement (see Buchanan 2000: 83).

Once this rudimentary statement of the need for shared norms is accepted, the second stage of constitutional choice, concerning the selection of the rules for political decision-making and of the constitutional limitations over the domain of politics, opens up. Here thesis (2), which points to the advantage of general rules and procedures over political discretion, can be fleshed out. The time horizon in which individuals make their choices impacts the degree of security they can expect. Moreover, both private and political interaction are thought of as sequential events, and not as one-shot games. This means that 'the individual is *uncertain* as to what his own precise role will be in any one of the whole chain of collective choices that will actually have to be made' (Buchanan and Tullock 1999: 78). The part of economic rationality that takes into consideration long-term scenarios is drawn to enter a setting akin to Rawls' (1971) veil of ignorance (see Brennan and Buchanan 2000: 155), where payoffs are not directly discernible by individuals because they cannot know what their actual interests will be.

On the one hand, Buchanan looks at the veil as embodying the classical liberal assumption of natural equality between persons (as highlighted by Peart and Levy 2020); on the other, he is reluctant to throw individual differences and maximizing behavior out of the picture, as he anchors the veil to the framework of rational choice. Although Buchanan often describes his philosophy as being at odds with Utilitarianism (see Buchanan and Tullock 1999: 15), the way he treats uncertainty in constitutional choice seems at times more in tune with Harsanyi's account than with Rawls' (the two are treated as analogous in Congleton and Buchanan 2003: 185–186). According to the former, in a situation of uncertainty, the usual economic motivational patterns take the shape of expected utility maximization mixed with an equiprobability judgement. The latter is the assumption that agents in a constitutional setting choose between alternative sets of rules by considering that 'under either system' they 'would have the same probability, 1/*n*, of taking the place of the best-off individual, or the second best-off individual, or the third best-off individual, etc., up to the worst-off individual' (Harsanyi 1976: 45), *n* being the total number of people in the political community.

To Buchanan, this setting leads to the selection of the principle of generality in legislation as opposed to discriminatory practices (compare Hayek 2011 to Congleton and Buchanan 2003): individuals would be sufficiently risk averse to avoid choosing an environment where political privileges exist and then participating in the lottery of life to fill one of the prospective winning positions. The idea of risk aversion also justifies a general scheme of redistribution as a form of social insurance (see Buchanan and Tullock 1999: 194–198). However, this conclusion does not lead Buchanan to accept something so strong as Rawls' principle of difference, as the latter implies that people would forego significant opportunities of gain in order to accommodate the set of institution which provides the least damaging worst-case scenario (see Harsanyi 1976: 39 ff.).

It is also in the light of the generality principle that the existence of democratic procedures, together with the element of representation, can be appreciated. Outside the domain of market interaction, democracy expresses the compromise between the effort to reduce external costs (both of private and public choices) *vis-à-vis* the costs embodied in the bargaining process to reach decisions (see Buchanan and Tullock 1999: 70–73). This by no means justifies an exclusive recourse of simple majority rule: it rather hints to the opportunity of assigning different sets of issues to different decision-making rules, according to their degree of impact on the general welfare.

Proposition (3) articulates further the antagonism between constitutionalism and discretionary power, this time tackling it from the side of political authority. Once the external enforcer is in place and background procedural mechanisms have been selected, there remains the task of effectively controlling Leviathan. In the time frame of ordinary politics, sectional incentives are available to players in all strata of society, including those who operate inside or at the borders of government. The activity of rent-seeking (see Tullock 2005) enlarges the domain of the public sector by targeted transfers or by creating legally privileged positions in the economy. Since this propension cannot be eliminated – pressure groups are coeval with political interaction – it has to be constrained, but this is difficult as long as government remains one centralized entity, even with the checks provided by the separation of powers.

This is precisely the departure point of the federalist argument that Buchanan and Tullock (see 1999: 24–25) seek to substantiate through economic theory. The Madisonian warning according to which 'ambition must be made to counteract ambition' (Hamilton et al. 2003: 252) is translated in practice by creating competition among smaller political units, supervised by a federal government with limited functions. On the one hand, the presence of multiple actors is a way to diffuse information in the system: if we frame policies as bundles of public goods and the citizen as a political consumer, we can see that the existence of alternative solutions may exert entrepreneurial pressures on governments towards acting more efficiently, thereby limiting the latter's invasiveness in public life. On the other, dividing up the territorial dimension of the monopoly of force reduces the costs of opting out to individuals, and this helps circumventing the problem of consent articulation, that is, of preference revelation about sub-rules of the political game (see Buchanan and Tullock 1999: 112–116; Ostrom 1987).

4. Political Realism and Contractarianism: The Two Souls of Public Choice

Taken together, the last two sections are descriptive of a tension which lies at the heart of public choice theory. One the one hand, its basic framework is a restatement of political realism through economic concepts. Agents are modeled as utility maximizers who compete to extract resources from the political process. The rents which are generated in this way differ from those that appear in the private sector: the latter tend to be dissipated by competition in a well-regulated market, but the former are not so easy to overthrow, as they are conditional on legal privileges (see Buchanan 1980). Moreover, while success in market competition is usually coupled with the production of added value for consumers and producers, the attempt to create rents through legislation involves a net waste in productive capacity, which is now redirected to the bargaining process with government. This complex of ideas is what, in Buchanan's terms, came to be known as 'politics without romance', or, after Tullock's (2005) studies, as 'the rent seeking society'. In this model, democratic politics is a matter of zero-sum games, where one player gains at the expense of the other. "General interest" now becomes a void notion, since every political measure that requires economic resources for its implementation, however inclusive in its conception, exerts sectional effects on different subsets of the population. As Arthur F. Bentley (1976, first published in 1908) noticed in *The Process of Government* – the first systematic treatise on interest groups in contemporary political theory – there is no overarching political or legal structure which is not the result of the underlying, contingent equilibrium of interest groups in a given society. One could say that the entire theory of coalitions (see Riker 1962) stems from Bentley's intuition, even after the latter has been corrected by Olson's (1965) theory of public goods – Olson himself, in his 1982 book *The Rise and Decline of Nations*, focuses on the pervasive impact of small and cohesive pressure groups on the economic life of Western democracies (Olson 1982: 74).

On the other hand, the constitutional theory outlined in Section 3 amounts to a wholly different picture of political relations: 'politics as exchange' (Buchanan 1987: 246). In *The Calculus of Consent*, Buchanan and Tullock state that the behavioral postulate of self-interest is not to be equated with the assumption that individuals seek to maximize the "power" they exercise over others (see Buchanan and Tullock 1999: 23–24). Reciprocal externalities must be treated as information, rather than as the embodiment of a real conflict: they signal that unrealized gains from trade exist. Accordingly, constitutions are seen as mechanisms that help people reach Pareto-optimal positions through private and public interaction. Of course, Buchanan and Tullock know that Pareto-optimality in collective choices is impossible to obtain through simple majority rule, because unanimity is the only way to verify that at least one member of the community is made better off by the transition from one social state to another, and no one is made worse-off. This is why Buchanan and Tullock (see 1999) introduce the crucial distinction between the constitutional stage, in which decision-making rules are selected, and actual in-period choices. They hold that, due to the condition of uncertainty regarding future positions, it is more likely that individuals will reach unanimous consent over a set of general rules, than over any particular question. By weighing decision-making costs against external costs, a constituency may agree to adopt less-than-unanimity rules for future interactions, thus encasing said rules in a contractarian justification: one cannot complain about a loss in a single iteration of a game if he has previously agreed to the rules. Still, Buchanan and Tullock show a sense of uneasiness towards simple majority rule, because, as I previously pointed out, they state that people would keep some matters out of its scope. For instance, they follow Wicksell (1896) in arguing that decisions concerning the fiscal structure of the polity would be assigned a qualified majority requirement.

There is nothing particularly original in pointing out the conflict between the two strands of public choice theory, as in recent times it has been the subject of scholarly work (to this effect see the collection of essays edited by Boettke and Stein 2018). However, the methodological nexus I have outlined between post-foundationalism and public choice in Section 1 is of help in better fleshing out the philosophical stakes of said tension. The ultimate source of the conflict between realism and constitutional political economy lies in the way they implement the principle of endogeneity, that is, the idea that institutions are not entities separated from society[3]. The first strand takes this principle

3 Economist Michele Boldrin has recently put into question the empirical validity of classical and contemporary liberal theories on the basis of this argument, and of the implications sketched in

to its logical conclusions, by stating that the interplay of interests in political life admits of no discontinuity based on different levels of decision-making. The picture is exactly the opposite than that painted by the veil of ignorance experiment, however designed. People in a constitutional setting are not risk averse precisely because they have a more or less definite ranking of objectives they hope to achieve by manipulating the rules of the game. They are willing to participate in the ensuing process of conflict and bargaining, and they are ready to try and overturn the result if it does not meet the expectations (compare Barry 1965: 200; De Jasay 1989: 96–109; Alves 2015), whether by way of ordinary politics or of constitutional interpretation (see De Jasay 1995: 205–214).

Moreover, as Brian Barry argues in his thorough critique of Buchanan and Tullock, the criterion of Pareto-optimality is unfit to describe political interaction, because it winds up depriving the latter of its essential feature: conflict based on moral principles. People do not cooperate by accepting the *status quo* distribution of resources as a neutral starting point from which to negotiate contracts. Rather, cooperation involves disagreement precisely over the legitimacy of each other's relative positions (see Barry 1965: 313). The rules-of-the-game approach to government is appropriate only for those rare cases where the only problem is to reach some equilibrium position, notwithstanding its content (see Barry 1965: 256). In all other instances, some kind of external decision is required to settle the matter. From a theoretical standpoint it is indifferent whether one, like Barry, chooses to see in this element of arbitration between claims a signal that the public interest as a meaningful concept can be identified, or whether one holds, like Pareto, that it belongs to the realm of 'non-logical action' (Pareto 1916: 63–196). The point is that no connection can be instituted between individual levels of welfare, mechanically considered, and the outcome of the political struggle (see Barry 1965: 52).

It is noteworthy that Buchanan and Tullock seem to be cognizant of the issues raised above. For instance, Buchanan, while discussing the flight from Hobbesian anarchy, looks at the initial *status quo* of the 'natural distribution' (Buchanan 2000: 75) as only *prima facie* legitimate. A conflict over the distribution of wealth is present *ab origine*, and the existence of a constitutional contract is conditional on it being addressed. In another passage, Buchanan and Tullock acknowledge that communities with wide internal differences along any social dimension will have a difficult time reaching agreement on

the following lines of the paragraph. Boldrin holds that all the different versions of this philosophical family – natural rights theories, accounts of cultural evolution, contractarianism – ultimately end up adopting the original position as a conceptual starting point, thus assuming away the problem of how to solve foundational conflicts. The "internal critique" of constitutional political economy outlined in the present paper can be regarded as a particular application of this general argument. Boldrin's position will be developed in a forthcoming book, titled *Inattualità del liberalismo*. A preliminary exposition of his ideas is available in an ongoing video series with the same title on Boldrin's Youtube channel.

general rules. These fractures can 'encourage the formation of predictable political coalitions', thereby leading to a permanent struggle, or to a situation where 'one of these coalitions has a clearly advantageous position at the constitutional stage' (Buchanan and Tullock 1999: 81). As a third and final point, one can say that the positive set of conclusions Buchanan and Tullock derive from their analysis of logrolling in the context of majority rule – namely the idea that logrolling is a way to enact the principle of compensation – is largely independent from the contractarian apparatus. If generalized, the central chapters of *The Calculus of Consent* present a version of 'politics as exchange' (Buchanan 1987: 246), that does not assume away actual individual interests.

Nevertheless, the conceptual tension remains. In other words, the project of constitutional political economy seems to take an awkward middle road between the two varieties of political theory outlined by Jon Elster (2003; also quoted by Colin-Jaeger et al. 2022: 117 in their comparison between Buchanan and Rawls): 'the market and the forum'. While the competitive theory of democracy and social choice theory blend the elements of exchange and conflict without making assumptions about what "true" individual preferences are, the ideal of "reasonableness" that permeates both the contractarian tradition and the theory of deliberative democracy puts significant weight on the possibility to give sectional interests a more agreeable shape by way of moral reflection and discussion.

5. Post-Foundationalism, Radical Democracy, and Social Choice

In Section 4, I undertook a critique of constitutional political economy through the post-foundational perspective. Here I will do the reverse exercise. Until now, I have mainly read post-foundationalism as a general attitude in positive political theory, which can be generalized well beyond the specific intellectual tradition(s) with which it is usually associated. As Marchart (see 2007: 3) remarks by referencing Oakeshott (see also Mouffe 2013: 109–114), one can come to see the fault in classical rationalism from many different starting points. However, one cannot ignore the recurrent link between post-foundationalism and a specific normative stance, that is, radical democracy. In what follows, I will try to show the shortcomings of this ideal by arguing that it dismisses too easily the "economic" reasons for a procedural order in a classical liberal-democratic sense *vis-a-vis* the nature of social choice.

Radical democracy can be defined as a conception of the democratic political form centred around the fact of pluralism and social antagonism. Rather than trying to eschew such pluralism by invoking supposedly shared ideas of justice, it holds that the vitality of democracy is signaled precisely by the irreducible conflict between conceptions of the good, which are as heterogeneous and changing as social identities themselves. Radical democracy is squarely opposed to the liberal understanding of public reason, as the latter refuses to acknowledge the double act of inclusion and exclusion inherent to any political choice (see Mouffe 2013: 91–102).

The concept of radical democracy can be read as the mature result of the twentieth-century encounter between Marxist theory and the Schmittian conception of the political. The latter contributed to updating the standard ideas about the priority of economic relations over political ones, by highlighting the role of political struggle as a subject-constituting event. Moreover, the antagonistic paradigm had the effect of generalizing the category of class struggle itself, as it allows for many different instances of conflict, which may be connected to, but also different from, the opposition between capitalists and the proletariat privileged by Marxist orthodoxy. The setting up of this new paradigm was also aided by the fabrication of a philosophical genealogy (on which see Portinaro 2018), which begins with Machiavelli and Spinoza and goes directly to Gramsci's theories of praxis and hegemony or to Foucault's analysis of power (the first two authors are championed in Antonio Negri's works – see Negri 1991, 1999 – while Gramsci's ideas were the key to the first development of the notion of radical democracy itself in Laclau and Mouffe 1985). The intention behind this work of interpretation is to trace an "alternative path" in modern thought, a path that severs the forces of democratization from the Enlightenment's faith in a form of universal reason (see Mouffe 2013: 93).

So described, the theory of radical democracy seems to amount to little more than a restatement of political realism, the only difference being that its main tenets are arrived at from a specific intellectual trajectory. One could pursue in more detail the path I outlined in Section 2 and pinpoint the common threads of development between the theory of antagonistic democracy and the theory of group interest in political science – for instance, both of them acknowledge the importance Marx's contribution, but look forward to overcoming its limitations (see Bentley 1976: 465 ff; Olson 1965: 102–110), and both of them owe a lot to elitist theory, either through the Schmittian or the Schumpeterian strand.

Nevertheless, one is left with the impression that radical democracy aims to take a step further. As Portinaro (see 2018) has observed, however, the direction is not always clear. The crux of the matter is the connection between political representation and proceduralism, towards which the proponents of radical democracy have an ambivalent attitude. On the one hand, theorists like Mouffe (see 1992: 1–16) and Esposito (see 2016, discussed in Portinaro 2018: 172–173) are careful in their formulation: they emphasize the break of the new paradigm with the totalitarian implication of State socialism (Esposito 2020 is especially clear on this point in his discussion of Lefort), and they claim to uphold the liberal democratic tradition in their intent to elaborate a richer concept of the citizen and of political participation. On the other, conceptions akin to Negri's (see 1999) constituent power point to a deeper fracture between orderly political structures and the dynamic force of social movements (see Portinaro 2018: 121). Either way, even if radical democracy does not *per se* coincide with the idealistic project of direct democracy or of a libertarian-socialist revolutionary order, it seems to entertain the same kind of mistrust towards fixed structures for the institutional mediation of conflict.

The priority accorded to spontaneous political praxis over constituted powers is the normative mirror double of the post-foundational hierarchy between "the political" and "politics". The main issue with this kind of 'hyperpoliticism' (Portinaro 2018: 72) can be found in the overall vagueness of the way it tackles the problem of organization – at the general level, not to be confused with the plane of political strategy. In other words, it is not particularly clear how the competition between opposing claims should be organized in a way that corrects the supposed shortcomings of representative democracy, while preserving pluralism at the same time. For instance, Mouffe looks at the option to radically extend the areas of economic equality as a way to better democratic participation. 'Defending and valuing the political form of society specific to liberal democracy does not commit us to the capitalist economic system' (Mouffe 1992: 2–3). Moreover, 'the various anti-capitalist struggles' are to be considered 'an integral part of the democratic revolution' (Mouffe 2013: 86). Whatever one thinks of the set of ideas in question, it is representative of a more general mistake: it appears that this kind of reasoning confuses the act of putting forward a specific claim in the struggle for hegemony with the analysis of a system of institutional rules for decision-making. If it is true that, in Rawlsian parlance, liberal constitutionalism fails to be inclusive enough, with its abstraction from particular conceptions of the good, a framework like the one now described does not really advance in making plurality manifest; on the contrary, it makes the latter conditional on the acceptance of an extremely demanding background arrangement.

It seems that we are back at the original contractarian conundrum: radical democracy, too, assumes away the problem of coordination. It insists on the manifold construction of social identities, but it also operates on the unspoken assumption that political commitment and group action are almost costless and do not vary based on selective incentives. Marchart partially admits this when, talking about Laclau and Mouffe, he says that radical democracy is not a necessary consequence of a post-foundationalist framework, but it is only 'one possible political project among others' (Marchart 2007: 176). On the other hand, it is not necessary, like proponents of radical democracy do, to equate the idea of procedural rationality with the Habermasian 'forum' perspective of deliberation. As Riker (1982) observes in his defence of the concept of 'Madisonian democracy', public/social choice theory has made clear, especially after Arrow's general impossibility theorem, that democratic procedures do not and cannot be used as gateways to the content of the "general will" or to the eventual harmonization of heterogeneous views of the world. They are coordinating mechanisms that allow to regulate the flow of social positions, that is, the competition between élites, and to control the action of political officials. The economic functions of constitutions I have described in Section 3, as well as the theory of political exchange, can be reframed in this perspective, without having to tap into the contractarian rationalization (see Ordeshook 1992).

6. Conclusions

I end by summarizing the main results of the present paper. (1) I have shown that the economic point of view on politics, far from constituting an essentialist position, can be regarded as post-foundationalist, because it shares with the autonomistic thesis an emergentist or criterion-oriented approach to social structures. (2) From here, I moved to the analysis of an important case where the economic approach actually blends with a foundationalist-contractarian stance: constitutional political economy. I argued that this paradigm is ripe with intellectual difficulties precisely in the spots where it tries to define a domain for rational agreement. (3) As a reverse exercise, I observed that radical democracy, which is usually associated with post-foundationalism, ends up replicating the same mistakes in its attempt to radicalize the idea of political antagonism. The general point of this paper was to show that a post-foundationalist outlook does not necessarily entail the demolition of constitutional and procedural rationality; on the contrary it can provide a pragmatic-economic justification of the latter.

Bibliography

Alves, A.A. (2015) 'No Salvation Through Constitution: Jasay Versus Buchanan and Rawls', *The Independent Review*, 20 (1), pp. 33–46.

Barry, B. (1965) *Political Argument*, London: Routledge & Kegan Paul.

Barry, B. (1978) *Sociologists, Economists and Democracy*, Chicago and London: The University of Chicago Press.

Becker, G.S. (1976) *The Economic Approach to Human Behavior*, Chicago and London: The University of Chicago Press.

Bentley, A.F. (1976) *The Process of Government: A Study of Social Pressures*, Cambridge, MA: Belknap Press.

Boettke, P.J., and Stein, S. (eds.) (2018) *Buchanan's Tensions: Reexamining the Political Economy and Social Philosophy of James M. Buchanan*, Arlington: Mercatus Center.

Brennan, G., and Buchanan, J.M. (2000) *The Reason of Rules: Constitutional Political Economy*, Indianapolis: Liberty Fund.

Buchanan, J.M. (1980) *Rent Seeking and Profit Seeking*, in Buchanan, J.M., Tollison R.D., and Tullock, G. (eds.), *Toward a Theory of the Rent-Seeking Society*, College Station: Texas A&M University Press, pp. 3–15.

Buchanan, J.M. (1987), 'The Constitution of Economic Policy', *The American Economic Review*, 77 (3), pp. 243–250.

Buchanan, J.M. (1999) *Cost and Choice: An Inquiry into Economic Theory*, Indianapolis: Liberty Fund.

Buchanan, J.M. (2000) *The Limits of Liberty: Between Anarchy and Leviathan*, Indianapolis: Liberty Fund.
Buchanan, J.M., and Tullock, G. (1999) *The Calculus of Consent: Logical Foundations of Constitutional Democracy*, Indianapolis: Liberty Fund.
Colin-Jaeger, N., Dold, M., and Gascoin, A. (2022) 'Realism and Deliberation in Normative Economics: The Fruitful Intellectual Dialogue Between James Buchanan and John Rawls', in Badiei, S., and Grivaux, G. (eds.), *The Positive and the Normative in Economic Thought*, London and New York: Routledge, pp. 108–128.
Congleton, R., and Buchanan, J.M. (2003) *Politics by Principle, Not Interest: Toward Nondiscriminatory Democracy*, Indianapolis: Liberty Fund.
De Jasay, A. (1989) *Social Contract, Free Ride: A Study of the Public Goods Problem*, Oxford: Clarendon Press.
De Jasay, A. (1995) *The State*, Indianapolis: Liberty Fund.
Downs, A. (1957) *An Economic Theory of Democracy*, New York: Harper & Row Publishers.
Elster, J. (2003) 'The Market and the Forum: Three Varieties of Political Theory', in Matravers, D., and Pike, J. (eds.), *Debates in Contemporary Political Philosophy: An Anthology*, London: Routledge, pp. 125–141.
Esposito, R. (2016) *Da fuori: una filosofia per l'Europa*, Torino: Einaudi.
Esposito, R. (2020) *Pensiero Istituente: Tre paradigmi di ontologia politica*, Torino: Einaudi.
Friedman, M. (1953) *Essays in Positive Economics*, Chicago and London: The University of Chicago Press.
Hamilton, A., Madison, J., and Jay, J. (2003) *The Federalist, with Letters of "Brutus"*, Cambridge: Cambridge University Press.
Harsanyi, J.C. (1976) *Essays on Ethics, Social Behavior, and Scientific Explanation*, Dordrecht: D. Reidel Publishing Company.
Hayek, F.A. (1948) *Individualism and Economic Order*, Chicago: The University of Chicago Press.
Hayek, F.A. (2011) *The Constitution of Liberty*, Chicago: The University of Chicago Press.
Laclau, E., and Mouffe, C. (1985) *Hegemony and Socialist Strategy: Towards a Radical Democratic Politics*, London: Verso.
Leoni, B. (2004) *Il diritto come pretesa*, Macerata: Liberilibri.
Marchart, O. (2007) *Post-Foundational Political Thought: Political Difference in Nancy, Lefort, Badiou and Laclau*, Edinburgh: Edinburgh University Press.
Masala, A. (2003), *Bruno Leoni*, Milano: Il Sole 24 Ore.
Mises, L.V. (1998) *Human Action: A Treatise in Economics*, Auburn: Ludwig von Mises Institute.
Mouffe, C. (1992) 'Democratic Politics Today', in *Dimensions of Radical Democracy: Pluralism, Citizenship, Community*, London: Verso.
Mouffe, C. (2013) *Hegemony, Radical Democracy, and the Political*, ed. by James Martin, London: Routledge.
Negri, A. (1991) *The Savage Anomaly: The Power of Spinoza's Metaphysics of Politics*, Minneapolis: University of Minnesota Press.

Negri, A. (1999) *Insurgencies: Constituent Power and the Modern State*, Minneapolis: University of Minnesota Press.

Nozick, R. (2013) *Anarchy, State, and Utopia*, New York: Basic Books.

Olson, M. (1965) *The Logic of Collective Action: Public Goods and the Theory of Groups*, Cambridge, MA: Harvard University Press.

Olson, M. (1982) *The Rise and Decline of Nations: Economic Growth, Stagflation, and Social Rigidities*, New Haven and London: Yale University Press.

Ordeshook, P.C. (1992) 'Constitutional Stability', *Constitutional Political Economy*, 3 (2), pp. 137–175.

Ostrom, E. (1990) *Governing the Commons: The Evolution of Institutions for Collective Action*, Cambridge: Cambridge University Press.

Ostrom, V. (1987) *The Political Theory of a Compound Republic: Designing the American Experiment*, Lincoln and London: University of Nebraska Press.

Pareto, V. (1916) *Trattato di sociologia generale. Volume 1*, Firenze: G. Barbera Editore.

Peart, S.J., and Levy, D.M. (2020) *Towards an Economics of Natural Equals: A Documentary History of the Early Virginia School*, Cambridge: Cambridge University Press.

Portinaro, P.P. (2018) *Le mani su Machiavelli: Una critica dell' "Italian Theory"*, Roma: Donzelli.

Rawls, J. (1971) *A Theory of Justice*, Cambridge, MA: Belknap Press.

Riker, W.H. (1962) *The Theory of Political Coalitions*, New Haven and London: Yale University Press.

Riker, W.H. (1982) *Liberalism Against Populism: A Confrontation Between the Theory of Democracy and the Theory of Social Choice*, Long Grove: Waveland Press Inc.

Robbins, L. (1984) *An Essay on the Nature and Significance of Economic Science*, London and Basingstoke: The Macmillan Press Ltd.

Schmitt, C. (2007) *The Concept of the Political: Expanded Edition*, Chicago and London: The University of Chicago Press.

Tullock, G. (2005) *The Rent-Seeking Society*, Indianapolis: Liberty Fund.

Weale, A. (2020) *Modern Social Contract Theory*, Oxford: Oxford University Press.

Wicksell, K. (1896) *Finanzteoretische Untersuchungen: Nebst Darstellung und Kritik des Steuerwesens Schwedens*, Jena: Verlag von Gustav Fischer.

5 The Crisis of Foundation and Democratic Representation

A Behavioral Perspective

Jacopo Marchetti

Introduction

A significant question within political philosophy is why certain forms of social order, like democracy, endure over time. There is a widespread consensus on the current challenges facing democratic systems and principles. Many scholars contend that Western democracies are struggling due to a declining trust in democratic norms, institutions, and political parties (Mair 2013; Merkel and Kneip 2018; Runciman 2018; Levitsky and Ziblatt 2018; Schäfer and Zürn 2023). Additionally, representative democracy is experiencing a crisis of representation, as contemporary party systems, which once played a vital role in shaping public opinion, have lost credibility (Lepoutre 2021). These trends are making democratic processes, public discourse, political deliberations, and compromises increasingly challenging. Models of deliberative democracy have been seen as a viable alternative to address the crisis facing traditional forms of democracy and representation. Over recent years, these models have gained considerable traction in academic debates, highlighting their potential to reshape democratic practices (see Fung 2020). However, according to a certain vein of the debate within the post-foundational constellation in continental philosophy, the visible signs of these phenomena are just the surface of a deeper crisis affecting the overall tradition of democracy and, precisely, the legitimacy of the realm of politics and its foundations. From this standpoint, the crisis stems from the fact that, beyond individuals that may be or not directly engaged in legal or political roles, the ideal of representation – and concepts such as "people", "political will" and "political representation" – while essential, do not correspond to any concrete, identifiable group or entity.

The Post-foundational Discourse Theory (PFDT) originally developed by Ernesto Laclau and Chantal Mouffe (see 2014) charges with the "consensus" model of democracy of suffering from idealization. It challenges the idea that political theory should seek foundational principles that are presumed to be universally valid and capable of establishing an ideal order; then it openly engages itself with the necessity to provide an empirical underpinning of

DOI: 10.4324/9781003471066-6

political principles. As Bissiato (2025) reminds in the Introduction, according to Mouffe, the need to identify some principles as ground of any orders must always deal with their ideal nature, that is, with the impossibility to find and constitute them in empirical reality. Because of its ideal nature which prevents the idea to enter into reality, the searching for stable principles that can ground the political world may be disappointing or unsatisfying. However, it does not mean that any searching would be useless, as the deconstructive approaches intend to show. This contribution aims to follow these insights and will provide justifications for embracing a new constructive perspective that can be seen as the flip side of post-foundational criticisms of democratic legitimacy: the behavioral approach, analogous to the successful field of research known as Behavioral Economics. This approach is situated at the crossroads between political epistemology and several branches of experimental, evolutionary, and behavioral sciences. The purpose is to understand how political and juridical dimensions can emerge from the different ways in which humans behave, organize, and utilize social knowledge, specifically to establish political principles based on the choices we make in various real political contexts. While in the first part the contribution offers an overview of the most "family members" of the post-foundational constellation, also highlighting some affinities between them and the social philosophy of the Austrian School (Sec. 1), in the remaining part it aims to compare the philosophical justifications offered by post-foundationalism with the behavioral underpinnings of human agency (Sec. 2) to offer a behavioral underpinning of social orders (Sec. 3) and of democratic institutions (Sec. 4).

1. Doing without Constructivism

In the course of history, political philosophers usually adopted a "constructivist" approach to seek out absolute, stable, or desirable principles that can ground a stable and, as possible, just society over time. The Hobbesian dimension represents one aspect of this line of thought. According to Hobbesian constructivism (see Hobbes 1996), to function effectively, the realm of politics must be grounded in some principles, such as some kind of justice, that someone is called to enforce. On the other hand, the normative tradition aims at identifying those principles that would be in people's interest to choose, but the source of normativity is usually borne by robust normative conceptions, no matter if the justification process meets the actual people's substantive conceptions of justice. An example of this is Rawls' *Theory of Justice* (TOJ), in which justice is understood as "fairness", beginning with the primacy of justice over the good (see Rawls 1999a). Conversely, the notion that the political and legal spheres can emerge without relying on established rational or normative principles appears to be at odds with the leading traditions in political philosophy.

From a methodological point of view, in almost all the reflections on the political meaning of order, the existence of institutions and social norms that regulate human behavior and explain cooperation is dismissed in a constructivist manner. Constructivism deliberately operates as a form of social constructivism, employing reason to deliberately establish rules that prescribe collective, purpose-oriented actions (see Hayek 1982; Smith 2003).

It suggests that the existence of institutions, rules, and social norms that regulate human behavior and explain cooperation would be a product of human design in compliance with reason, through which they can be discovered. Constructivism has long dominated within continental and realist philosophy, and its more exemplary formulation is Thomas Hobbes' *Leviathan*. In his view, likewise the prisoner's dilemma situation, individuals need to cooperate to survive, but groups cannot spontaneously secure collective decisions (see McLean 1981; Taylor 1976; Sugden 1990). The institution of the Commonwealth is compared to a public good that only the sovereign with the monopoly and use of coercion can provide (see Hardin 1991). According to Hobbesian constructivism, the obedience of the subjects to the law requires embracing some kind of justice that can simply be achieved via reason. Moreover, the authority is functional to its creation and its subsistence over time: natural laws exist beyond the legal production as "product of the mind", but without any authority that acts as a third party to enforce contracts, respect, and sanction defectors, conflicts cannot be avoided. In other words, legal rules *can yet be rationally discovered, but not rationally practicable.*

During the years, constructivism, along with the consensus model of democracy as one of its potential theoretical applications, have drawn many adversaries. Among them, it can be placed the Scottish Enlightenment's social philosophy (see Hayek 1988; Smith 1998, 2009; Otteson 2007), F.A. Hayek's political epistemology and his idea of Spontaneous Order (see Hayek 1982) and Michael Oakeshott's idea that political activity is ungrounded insofar it always enfolded in sedimented layers of traditions which evolve in time (see Oakeshott 1991). In recent times, PFDT has revived these criticisms and developed them independently, offering a constructive explanation that stands in contrast to the deconstructive approaches commonly promoted in continental philosophy.

Originally formulated as a critique of Political Economy aimed at deconstructing the essentialist foundations of Marxism, PFDT confronts the fundamental issue of political foundation by engaging with the works of Carl Schmitt, John Rawls, and Jürgen Habermas (see Mouffe 1999). PFDT rests on two main pillars: constructive explanations and discursive practices. To begin with, it questions the pursuit of universal, ideal principles as the basis for social and political order. One of its main contributions consist of exposing the fragility of our social foundations and the burdens they place on otherness. Instead, it suggests a heightened awareness of contingency, understood as the point of partial and, ultimately, inevitably unsuccessful grounding. However, PFDT must not be confused with the anti-foundational thinking; while it recognizes that specific foundations are always constructed and contingent, it does not deny the existence of foundations themselves neither to erase completely such figures of the ground. The unnecessity of grounding orders and rules on metaphysical figures of foundation – such as totality, universality, essence is not equivalent to "anything goes". What is being challenged is the assumption that an ultimate foundation is impossible, but it can be expressed in contingent and regular practice that emphasizes how language and other forms of communication shape and constitute social reality. According to this view, discourses are not just about representing reality but are central to the construction of social and political identities and power relations. This represents a constructive explanation, in contrast to the purely deconstructive approaches found in hermeneutics and postmodernism, which argue that, since there is no ultimate foundation, one must confront the very abyss that serves as its ground.

It is rarely acknowledged that, although not employing the same arsenal of topoi, nor sharing the same viewpoints and languages, PFDT reaches conclusions very similar to those of Oakeshott (see Marchart 2007; Gurhanli 2013), and certain proponents of the Austrian School tradition. Oakeshott's "bottomless abyss" figure serves as a metaphor for a foundation that cannot be anchored or established to any fixed point (see Marchart 2007: 3). Oakeshott and post-foundational thinkers agree that political activity is unfounded as it does not take place in a vacuum, but it is grounded in traditions which are not goal-oriented. On the other hand, Hayek's notion of social institutions as something rooted in human behavior, culturally set and evolutionary shaped, replaces the attention of contingency that is pivotal in the post-foundation thought. Recognizing the existence of institutions that are neither the product of a deliberate plan nor require a foundation rooted in something endogenous to the political realm has always been a challenge for the human being, since it went beyond the scope of his own mind. This view is 'rooted originally in a deeply ingrained propensity of primitive thought to interpret all regularity to be found in phenomena anthropomorphically, as the result of the design of a thinking mind' (Hayek 1982: 9). Carl Menger, who inspired Hayek's political epistemology and his theory of Spontaneous Order, was perfectly aware of this when he wrote his method of the social sciences (see Menger 2009) many years before complexity theories were fixed in the scientific debate. Almost 140 years have passed since the first publication of that book, and more than half a century since its diffusion in the non-German-speaking world, and many of the statements contained therein demonstrate a surprising topicality that can trigger the scholarly debate on political foundation. In the meantime, the study of complex problems has required a growing interdisciplinarity between the different disciplines, and for many of the intuitions that until a century ago remained conjectures, it is now possible to find a foundation empirically.

Several branches of economic and social science, including field experimental economics and behavioral economics, today are sympathetic to these insights. This body of research represents the culmination of a path that began with Menger's method and Hayek's social philosophy. At first glance, it may seem difficult to identify a continuity between the behavioral approach and the Austrian method of economics as an a priori science. Indeed, Menger conceived of "practical economic science" as a subfield of economic science, whose objectives were to determine general forms, typical relations, and the laws governing phenomena. As such, it excluded any attempt to prove social behavior through experiments in the same way that the "exact" natural sciences do (see Cevolani 2011).

However, recent research in behavioral economics has (albeit not always intentionally) triggered insights from the Austrian tradition by testing its theses through experimentation (see Frantz and Leeson 2013). This research combines cognitive psychology, evolutionary biology, and behavioral decision theory to enhance the analysis of political institutions (see Teraji 2018). The idea that experimental results can contribute to the development of concepts for prescriptive analysis is valuable in adopting a behavioral perspective on political and social foundations. The following section of the contribution will attempt to clarify what a behavioral approach to these questions would consist of and why it can integrate some issues raised by PFDT.

2. Normativity and Philosophical Justifications

PFDT offers constructive explanations that aim to fill the "void" left by deconstructive perspectives, which contend that seeking any political foundation is fundamentally unrealizable. However, the shift from critique to concrete models has consistently fallen short of expectations, a challenge exemplified by Mouffe's work (see Wingenbach 2016: xi). Agonistic democracy (see Mouffe 2000a) represents one possible application and forms the constructive part of those explanations. It has been presented as being hostile to normative models of liberal democracy, such as John Rawls' political liberalism (see Rawls 2005), as it involves engaging in reflective self-critique that highlights the contingency of social structures and expands opportunities for the inclusion of diverse identities in ways that political liberalism is not successful in achieving. PFDT accuses the consensus model of democracy of abstractionism, as it offers universally valid concepts (such as justice and freedom) which, in reality, regulate individual interests in a way that conforms to the authors' idea of democracy, rather than presenting those concepts as shaped by specific cultural and historical contexts. According to PFDT, Rawls (as well as other models of consensus democracy, such as Habermas') suggest that political principles, at least in theory, can be harmonized through a consensus reached by free and equal citizens exchanging public reasons (see also Rawls 1997). However, when put into practice, this ideal of reconciliation becomes a paradox: 'liberal democracy is precisely the recognition of this constitutive gap between the people and its various identifications', which attempts to fill this gap through the establishment of a 'supposedly rational" consensus' (Mouffe 2000b: 56) that serves as its foundation. Obviously, this does not mean that agonistic democracy is fully at odds with political liberalism (for example, Wingenbach insists that political liberalism can emerge as an institutional model for agonistic democracy). Rather, they identify the sources of normativity at different levels.

To gain a clearer understanding of this question, we can view it through the lens of Robert Nozick's philosophical justifications (see Nozick 2017). In a general sense, a philosophical explanation predicts the conditions of possibility of certain facts or events P. Philosophical justification, instead, must build a justification of the event P if "P" is accepted as recognized as valid by all the subjects involved in it. In this sense, we achieve a normative philosophical justification. Normative theory is independent in their normative claims from descriptions of reality: what drives normative issues is always an Archimedean point, usually consisting of a hypothetical situation that is deemed desirable. This argument is built on a philosophical justification.

A significant amount of discussion in normative political theory revolves around arguments similar to the search for philosophical justification. These discussions center on the validity of these principles or claims, where "truth" is defined not by access to normative or ontological reality but by the upshot of a supposed democratic consensus among "like us" reasonable and rational individuals who view themselves as free and equal moral agents. Hence, the efforts of normative theory are compromised by their alignment with the concepts of "democracy" and "democratic" agent (such as the individual inspired by the virtue of reasonableness) outlined by the philosopher in question, which ultimately hides her or his particular viewpoint on these matters. In that case, where does the source of normativity come from? It seems that even if certain basic principles cannot exist, the process of justifying those principles involves a top-down approach to normativity that grounds them. Instead, the post-foundational approach to political theory asserts that any normative justification for a set of coherent political claims will always have at its core a tacit (and more or less arbitrary) social agreement that is contingent and necessary, but that can never be fully representative of the flesh-and-blood political subjects, neither normatively assume ex ante. Social agreement is incompatible with any top-down model of consensus: it is fugacious and culturally situated; it lives into practices.

Obviously, the methodological backgrounds, tools, and languages employed by behavioral and post-foundational approaches are very different: while PFDT places its reflection within the problem of political foundation and the category of the political, a behavioral approach is guided by underlying cognitive and epistemically determined factors that underpin human behavior. On one side, the focus is on the problem of contingency, and the forms of empirical reality embedded in practices; on the other side, we have the patterns of behavior of flesh-and-blood agents. If we introduce a behavioral framework we substitute the problem of foundation with the question of underpinning. Despite drawing from very different intellectual lineages, the behavioral approach discussed in this contribution shares some common premises with post-foundational criticisms of foundation: 1) tracing ontological foundations and their metaphysical status back to concrete reality, that is, reducing political principles to the empirical reality of practices and behaviors; 2) the impossibility of precisely identifying *how* and *where* a social order emerges, even though we serve it and sometimes benefit from it. Moreover, both of these approaches inveigh against the idea of top-down normativity, specifically the fact that even when presented as not ontologically or normatively determined, political principles always conceal a normatively grounded ex ante, which often coincides with that of the philosopher.

A behavioral approach to democracy cannot accept that its principles and conditions should be defined by normative assumptions (e.g., the idea that people act in compliance with the ideal of public reason, even when they do not, or that justice as fairness is the most appropriate political principle that reasonable and rational agents would choose). Normative philosophical justifications parallel Milton Friedman's famous "as if" clause (see Friedman 1953), which asserts that (economic) theory remains valid regardless of the type of rationality exhibited by real agents. In that case, the goal was to construct a model and assess the hypothesis based on its explanatory power, rather than how people actually behave. A hypothesis is valuable if it explains much with little, meaning it abstracts the essential elements from the complexity of surrounding circumstances and allows for valid predictions based on those key factors alone. On the contrary, a behavioral approach cannot accept the idea that democracy has an intrinsic foundation. It seeks to establish political principles based on the choices we make in various real political contexts: it does this by considering specific types of behavior as reflective of particular choices, which are then viewed as indicative of certain political preferences (see Floyd 2020). These preferences are regarded as expressions of, and foundations for, political principles, as their viability is established only when institutions can be designed to be acceptable to people as they are. Building on Guala's concerns (see 2021), a behavioral approach should design institutions while considering people *as they are*, rather than *as if they are* (or as philosophers would prefer them to be). Such institutions should not be implemented based on either descriptive or normative claims.

3. A Behavioral Underpinning of Social Order

As discussed earlier, a behavioral approach must refrain from assuming a normative theory that determines which political principles allegedly rational and reasonable agents would be best positioned to choose, nor should it assume that those principles are definitive and universally valid. A clear example of this way of thinking is represented by Rawls's TOJ clauses on the choice of principles of justice, namely that the principles must satisfy the requirements of universality in application and finality (i.e., they are regarded as the final court of appeal, as the choice cannot be revised once it is made). On the contrary, a behavioral approach should frame the problem of foundation as an "institutional problem" through the lens of a problem-solving activity (see Newell and Simon 1972). Every social problem-solving process begins with framing about certain aspects of society (P). The problem description typically singles out a state of affairs that is wanted to be achieved by specified agents. PFDT 'describes the position that human beings require meaning in order to make sense of the world, and that the constructions of meaning that dominate a particular time or culture serve as foundational narratives for social life' (Wingenbach 2016: xvi); similarly, a behavioral approach would focus on how political and legal dimensions emerge from the different ways humans act, organize, and apply social knowledge.

One of the primary questions a behavioral approach should focus on is the source of the bonds within a social order. We live surrounded by legal institutions, constraints, and social norms that help human decision-makers carry out the myriad coordination tasks they encounter in everyday life yet often take for granted. Where do they come from? Questions about how an order is established, why it endures over time, and how it evolves are peripheral to the core debate within the leading traditions of political philosophy.

Understanding the interaction between different types of norms is fundamental to grasping how various political orders take shape, evolve, and either succeed or fail. However, attempting to solve the age-old problem in social sciences – namely, the causal links between agents, structures, and institutions – has proven to be a dead-end strategy, to the extent that it has been likened to the chicken-and-egg dilemma (see Nozick 1977). Those who have sought to unpack this long-standing debate quickly realize the strong polarization between methodological approaches across disciplines, which has long hindered communication between them. The untranslatability of micro-level findings into aggregate terms, along with the inaccuracies of holistic descriptions of individual strategic behavior, has contributed to opposing these disciplines based on their respective research methods. For example, the debate in sociology has been split between advocates of holism and those of methodological individualism (see Parri 2014). The former – which includes not only methodological positivism but also functionalism, structuralism, and ethnomethodological approaches – examines the normative factors within institutional contexts by focusing on how rules constrain and enable the behavior of individuals and groups. The latter, on the other hand, explains social phenomena by starting from individual action and its capacity to generate stable and interactive structures, which are then formalized as norms.

However, some of the criticisms – perhaps the most constructive – leveled against methodological individualism do not concern the alleged atomistic fallacy, which is easy to refute given the formal weakness of the hypotheses, but instead focus on the level of causal explanation. Methodological individualism has been criticized for oversimplifying the complexity of social phenomena: it offers a one-sided explanation, privileging the effects of individual actions on the social order as a whole (see Di Iorio 2016). As a result, 'the influence of the whole upon the parts is simply as a constraint upon or an input to a pre-given function, not a change in the function itself' (Hodgson 1988: 54–55).

In contrast to this approach, we can adopt a third way: methodological cognitivism (see Viale 2013). This approach centers on the cognitive features of the agent, emphasizing how the mind interprets social phenomena by considering both ontogenetic characteristics (such as imperfect beliefs and mental models) and phylogenetic factors (such as cultural inheritance and moral psychology). Once combined with research on the socially extended mind (see Gallagher 2013; Gallagher and Petracca 2020) and embodied bounded rationality (see Gallese et al. 2020; Gigerenzer 2021), it demonstrates how social interaction engages agents in a dynamic interplay with their environment, even in contexts of deep uncertainty, shaping their cognition while preserving their relational autonomy in the world. Scaffolding Institutions a feature particular conditions that arise from people's responses to the environment; this is their underpinning. Therefore, understanding how social actors will use knowledge to exploit current opportunities is critical for grasping the different paths of change within institutional contexts. From this perspective, Individuals and institutions are not reducible to one another: institutions are essential for guiding individual actions but do not entail "situational determinism".

Additionally, although beliefs are based on a personal dimension related to an individual's life history and past experiences, they draw strength from both the cultural context in which they take shape and a social dimension that arises from the long cultural evolution of the human species (see Boyd and Richerson 2005; Henrich et al. 2005; Bowles and Gintis 2011). The initial architecture of the structure is genetic, but 'the subsequent scaffolding is a result of the experiences of the individual – experiences coming from the physical environment and from the socio-cultural linguistic environment' (North 2005: 25). An institutional framework for understanding the interdependency between individuals, their foundations, and culture is Constitutional Culture. This framework has been utilized to examine beliefs, cultural models, and the cognition of national identities that are embedded in both informal and formal constraints, manifested through tacit knowledge and implicit interests (Wenzel 2010). In other words, both legal norms and informal constraints of society are 'culture-specific' (Boettke 1996; Grube and Storr 2015) in the sense that culture can serve as the lens through which individuals interpret and make sense of their actions, opportunities, environment and, ultimately, process the world (see also Geertz 1973). This is an aspect that has widely emerged in PFDT's criticism of foundationalism.

4. A Behavioral Approach to Democracy: Some Insights

The final section of the contribution discusses what a practical behavioral approach to democracy entails, emphasizing that its underpinning should be how individuals understand the social bonds that surround them. As mentioned, a behavioral underpinning of democracy should imagine institutions based on the current epistemic assumptions of agents, meaning that these institutions should be designed with a foundation in human factors (which include cognitive and culturally situated components through which institutions are constantly shaped). In this sense, institutions should be acceptable to people *as they are*.

To clarify this point, let's go back to Rawls' TOJ. Rawls seeks to eliminate any teleological (and theological) assumptions and rejects any metaphysical justification for political principles (of justice). He claims that 'conceptions of justice must be justified by the conditions of our life as we know it' (Rawls 1999a/1999b: 454). Indeed, a significant portion of his TOJ is dedicated to conceiving governing principles of society that can be accepted by its members. The same can be inferred from one of his later works, wherein he coined the term "realistic utopia" to align his theory with the contingent reality of things (see Rawls 1999b). Despite Rawls' aims to identify institutions that are in people's best interest to choose, this interest is driven by a robust normative understanding of the epistemic goods democracy should defend, particularly the ideas of fairness and the primacy of justice over notions of the good. Who can determine that these characteristics are fundamental epistemic goods for people? The principles that individuals would accept under the veil of ignorance should align with the realities of human psychology, rather than being derived from universal principles that underpin politics or normatively imposed based on what Rawls claims people would choose (such as the liberal egalitarian principle that prioritizes the disadvantaged). For instance, he argues that the principle of difference is more aligned with actual human moral psychology than alternatives such as utilitarianism. What grounds does he use to draw conclusions about real human moral psychology? How can we be certain that liberal egalitarianism is the option real people would choose? For example, it is possible that individuals might favor a system of "natural liberty" over liberal egalitarianism. Behavioral sciences can help us address this question. Experimental evidence may provide insights into the cognitive processes that lead to one judgment over another. If individuals in a similar setup choose different principles than those selected by representatives in the original position, this suggests that Rawls may be mistaken about the rationality of the principles and people's. Paradoxically, even if primary goods must be satisfied in a certain way, it is possible for people to prefer having less rather than more.

Typically, in applied work, the economist-scientist operates within a controlled framework, such as field experiments, to understand the effects of specific measures or policies on particular outcomes (see Guala 2005). There are important methodological differences within applied and experimental behavioral research (see Di Cagno et al. 2023), but, in general terms, an ideal causal experiment involves the controlled manipulation of a variable while holding other potentially relevant factors constant. By adjusting the presumed cause, we can ascertain that the observed outcome results from this manipulation rather than from other factors that may typically coincide with the variation (see Mize and Manago 2022). A similar approach can be envisioned when designing political institutions.

While experimental methods are encouraged in scholarly debates on politics, they often lack a unified and consolidated methodology (see Lindauer 2023). Indeed, there are various interpretations of experimental designs. For instance, among the possible alternatives among the possible conceptions of democracy, the idea of experimental democracy has recently emerged. It utilizes experimental architecture to identify effective means of addressing issues through deliberation and active citizen participation in policy adoption. This approach frequently employs tools of deliberative democracy, such as mini-publics, deliberative polls, and citizen juries (see Fung 2007). In this framework, voting determines which tentative solutions to pursue or test. Citizens are incentivized to engage with the res publica, set moral boundaries for the experiments, and identify the most suitable policies for specific contexts. Naturally, this would require engaging in the long-running debate about voters' competence – specifically, what skills voters should possess to be considered competent. However, this is not the direction this contribution intends to take, as within the framework of experimental democracy, citizens actively participate in the policy design process through "one vote each". Using Esther Duflo's metaphor, in a behavioral democracy, the role of the experimenter resembles the economist as a *plumber*. Duflo (see 2017) argues that through her plumber's kit, the economist helps identify critical details that explain the relationship between policy and outcomes in specific contexts. The economist aims to install a "machine" in the real world through observation and adapts the design before scaling it up. When applying a behavioral approach to democracy, philosophers can not only draw on experimental results in their research but also participate in designing and conducting experiments. In local, small-scale experiments within a group or community, a designer can determine which experimental move to make first and subsequently assess and evaluate the consequences of various rule changes (i.e., the social experiment). This suggestion aligns with Thrasher's (see 2023) experimental political philosophy, which emphasizes the need to pursue political questions while taking empirical inquiry seriously. Thrasher argues that conducting empirical research to assess the effectiveness of normative concepts should be an active endeavor for moral and political philosophers (see also Lindauer 2020); they must 'be actively involved in conducting empirical research that will help us ascertain whether particular normative concepts are fruitful' (Lindauer 2020:

2148). Behavioral lab experiments and empirical evidence are valuable not only for developing the material needed to clarify political concepts but also for testing the effectiveness of revisionary concepts.

Final Remarks

This contribution has examined the long-standing issue of political foundation in light of the alleged crisis of democratic representation highlighted in recent scholarly debates. According to a certain perspective within continental philosophy, this crisis arises from the intrinsic inadequacy of political and theoretical concepts to address the contingent nature of the empirical realm of politics. PFDT provides an innovative – though at times blurred in its pars construes – analysis of the impossibility of finding a stable ground for politics. The contribution emphasized that post-foundational critiques of foundationalism have independently revived some elements within the Austrian School's reflections on the nature of social orders, particularly Hayek's idea of Spontaneous Order. In its constructive part, the contribution aimed to provide an interpretation of these questions to offer a behavioral underpinning of social order and democratic institutions. Can a sense of the political world be established? A behavioral approach can address some points that post-foundational criticisms have left inconclusive on the practical side. It shows that legal institutions, as well as social norms, can emerge from the ways social agents interpret their world through dynamic and reciprocal interactions with ontogenetic and phylogenetic qualities and their environment. Additionally, some insights have been offered that point towards a behavioral approach to democracy. They suggest that we should ground institutions that align with the interests, preferences, and behaviors of real people on the basis of evidence and experimental settings to provide a more comprehensive understanding of the factors involved in individual and collective choices. Certainly, political philosophers often hesitate to engage with behavioral and experimental considerations, and they typically do not adopt the fundamental empirical methods of the behavioral sciences. Moreover, deconstructive and constructive perspectives seldom interact with disciplines outside their own. But the suggestions of this contribution may provide insights for future research directions.

Bibliography

Bissiato, G. (2025) 'Introduction', in Bissiato G. (ed.) *Law, Democracy and the Crisis of Foundation: Deconstructive and Constructive Perspectives*, London: Routledge.

Boettke, P.J. (1996) 'Why Culture Matters: Economics, Politics and the Imprint of History', *Amagi: The Journal of the Hayek Society at the London School of Economics*, 2 (1), pp. 9–16.

Bowles, S., and Gintis, H. (2011) *A Cooperative Species: Human Reciprocity and Its Evolution*, Princeton and Oxford: Princeton University Press.

Boyd, R., and Richerson, P.J. (2005) *Not by Genes Alone: How Culture Transformed Human Evolution*, Chicago and London: The University of Chicago Press.
Cevolani, G. (2011) 'Hayek in the Lab: Austrian School, Game Theory, and Experimental Economics', *L&PS*, 9 (1), pp. 429–436.
Di Cagno, D., Güth, W., and Sillari, G. (2023) 'The Better Toolbox: Experimental Methodology in Economics and Psychology', *Mind & Society*, 12 (1), pp. 53–66.
Di Iorio, F. (2016) 'Introduction: Methodological Individualism, Structural Constraints, and Social Complexity', *Cosmos+Taxis*, 3 (2), pp. 1–8.
Duflo, E. (2017) 'The Economist as Plumber', *American Economic Review*, 101 (5), pp. 1–26.
Floyd, J. (2020) 'Normative Behaviourism as a Solution to Four Problems in Realism and Non-Ideal Theory', *Critical Review of International Social and Political Philosophy*, 23 (2), pp. 137–162.
Frantz, R., and Leeson, R. (eds.) (2013) *Hayek and Behavioral Economics*, London: Palgrave Macmillan.
Friedman, M. (1953) *Essay in Positive Economics*, Chicago: The University of Chicago Press.
Fung, A. (2007) 'Minipublics: Deliberative Designs and Their Consequences', in Rosenberg, S.W. (ed.), *Deliberation, Participation and Democracy: Can the People Govern?* Basingstoke: Palgrave Macmillan, pp. 159–183.
Fung, A. (2020) 'Afterword: Does Deliberative Democracy Have a Role in Our Time of Political Crisis?', *Journal of Deliberative Democracy*, 16 (1), pp. 75–76.
Gallagher, S. (2013) 'The Socially Extended Mind', *Cognitive System Research*, 25–26, pp. 4–12.
Gallagher, S., and Petracca, E. (2020) 'Economic Cognitive Institutions', *Journal of Institutional Economics*, 16 (6), pp. 747–765.
Gallese, V., Mastrogiorgio, A., Petracca, E., and Viale, R. (2020) 'Embodied Bounded Rationality', in Viale, R. (ed.), *Routledge Handbook of Bounded Rationality*, London and New York: Routledge, pp. 377–390.
Geertz, C. (1973) *The Interpretation of Cultures: Selected Essays*, New York: Basic Books.
Gigerenzer, G. (2021) 'Embodied Heuristics', *Frontiers in Psychology*, 12, pp. 1–12.
Grube, L. E., Storr. H. V. (2015) (ed.) *Culture and economic action*, Cheltenham, Northampton: Elgar.
Guala, F. (2005) *The Methodology of Experimental Economics*, Cambridge: Cambridge University Press.
Guala, F. (2021) 'Behavioural Politics: Social Insurance and Mutual Benefit in Robert Sugden's the Community of Advantage', *International Review of Economics*, 68 (1), pp. 89–100.
Gurhanli, H. (2013) 'Post-Foundationalism of Laclau and Oakeshott: Politics of Faith, Skepticism and Populism', *Annales Philosophici*, 7, pp. 26–37.
Hardin, R. (1991) 'Hobbesian Political Order', *Political Theory*, 19 (2), pp. 156–180.
Hayek, F.A. (1982) *Law, Legislation and Liberty: A New Statement of the Liberal Principles of Justice and Political Economy*, London: Routledge & Kegan.

Hayek, F.A. (1988) *The Fatal Conceit: The Errors of Socialism*, ed. by W.W. Bartley III, London: Routledge.

Henrich, J., Boyd, R., Bowles, S., Camerer, C., Fehr, E., Gintis, H., McElreath, R., Alvard, M., Barr, A., Ensminger, J., Smith Henrich, N., Hill, K., Gil-White, F., Gurven, M., Marlowe, F.W., Patton, J.Q., and Trace, D. (2005) 'Models of Decision-Making and the Coevolution of Social Preferences', *Behavioral and Brain Sciences*, 28 (6), pp. 838–855.

Hobbes, T. (1996) *Leviathan*, ed. with an intro. by J.C.A. Gaskin, Oxford: Oxford University Press.

Hodgson, G.M. (1988) *Economics and Institutions: A Manifesto for a Modern Institutional Economics*, Cambridge: Polity Press.

Laclau, E., and Mouffe, C. (2014) *Hegemony and Socialist Strategy: Towards a Radical Democratic Politics*, vol. 8, Verso Books.

Lepoutre, M. (2021) *Democratic Speech in Divided Times*, Oxford University Press.

Levitsky, S., and Ziblatt, D. (2018) *How Democracies Die: What History Reveals About Our Future*, New York: Crown.

Lindauer, M. (2020) 'Experimental Philosophy and the Fruitfulness of Normative Concepts', *Philosophical Studies*, 177 (8), pp. 2129–2152.

Lindauer, M. (ed.) (2023) *Advances in Experimental Political Philosophy*, Bloomsbury Academic.

Mair, P. (2013) 'The Challenge to Party Government', in Goetz, K.H., Mair, P., and Smith, G. (eds.), *European Politics: Pasts, Presents*, London and New York: Routledge, pp. 211–234.

Marchart, O. (2007) *Post-foundational political thought: political difference in Nancy, Lefort, Badiou & Laclau*, Edinburgh: Edinburgh University Press.

McLean, I. (1981) 'The Social Contract in Leviathan and the Prisoner's Dilemma Supergame', *Political Studies*, 29 (3), pp. 339–351.

Menger, C. (2009) *Investigations into the Method of the Social Sciences*, Auburn, AL: Mises Institute.

Merkel, W., and Kneip, S. (2018) *Democracy and Crisis: Challenges in Turbulent Times*, Cham: Springer.

Mize, T.D., and Manago, B. (2022) 'The Past, Present, and Future of Experimental Methods in the Social Sciences', *Social Science Research*, 108.

Mouffe, C. (1999) 'Deliberative Democracy or Agonistic Pluralism?', *Social Research*, 66 (3), pp. 745–758.

Mouffe, C. (2000a) 'For an Agonistic Model of Democracy', in Sullivan, O. (ed.), *Political Theory in Transition*, London: Routledge, pp. 113–130.

Mouffe, C. (2000b) *The Democratic Paradox*, Verso.

Newell, A., and Simon, H.A. (1972) *Human Problem Solving*, Englewood Cliffs: Prentice-Hall.

North, D.C. (2005) *Understanding the Process of Economic Change*, Princeton and Oxford: Princeton University Press.

Nozick, R. (1977) 'On Austrian Methodology', *Synthese*, 36 (3), pp. 353–392.

Nozick, R. (2017) *Anarchy, State, and Utopia*, Malden, Oxford and Carlton: Blackwell.

Oakeshott, M. (1991) *On Human Conduct*, Oxford: Clarendon Press.

Otteson, J.R. (2007) 'Unintended Order Explanations in Adam Smith and the Scottish Enlightenment', in Hunt, L., and McNamara, P. (eds.), *Liberalism,*

Conservatism, and Hayek's Idea of Spontaneous Order, New York: Palgrave Macmillan, pp. 21–41.
Parri, L. (2014) *Explanation in the Social Sciences: A Theoretical and Empirical Introduction*, Soveria Mannelli: Rubbettino.
Rawls, J. (1997) 'The Idea of Public Reason Revisited', *The University of Chicago Law Review*, 64 (3), pp. 765–807.
Rawls, J. (1999a) *A Theory of Justice*, Cambridge, MA: The Belknap Press of Harvard University Press.
Rawls, J. (1999b) *The Law of Peoples: With the Idea of Public Reason Revisited*, Cambridge, MA: Harvard University Press, 2001.
Rawls, J. (2005) *Political Liberalism*, New York: Columbia University Press.
Runciman, D. (2018) *How Democracy End*, Basic Books.
Schäfer, A., and Zürn, M. (2023) *The Democratic Regression: The Political Causes of Authoritarian Populism*, John Wiley & Sons.
Smith, C. (2009) 'The Scottish Enlightenment, Unintended Consequences and the Science of Man', *Journal of Scottish Philosophy*, 7 (1), pp. 9–28.
Smith, V.L. (1998) 'The Two Faces of Adam Smith', *Economic Journal*, 65 (1), pp. 1–19.
Smith, V.L. (2003) 'Constructivist and Ecological Rationality in Economics', *American Economic Review*, 93 (3), pp. 465–508.
Storr, V.H., and John, A. (2020) *Cultural Considerations within Austrian Economics*, Cambridge: Cambridge University Press.
Sugden, R. (1990) 'Contractarianism and Norms', *Ethics*, 100 (4), pp. 768–786.
Taylor, M. (1976) *Anarchy and Cooperation*, London: Wiley.
Teraji, S. (2018) *The Cognitive Basis of Institutions: A Synthesis of Behavioral and Institutional Economics*, London: Academic Press.
Thrasher, J. (2023) 'Experimental Political Philosophy: A Manifesto', in Lindauer, M. (ed.), *Advances in Experimental Political Philosophy*, Bloomsbury Academic, pp. 237–257.
Viale, R. (2013) *Methodological Cognitivism*, 2 vols., Heidelberg: Springer.
Wenzel, N. (2010) 'From contract to mental model: Constitutional culture as a fact of the social sciences', *The Review of Austrian Economics*, 23, pp. 55–78.
Wingenbach, E. (2016) *Institutionalizing agonistic democracy: Post-foundationalism and political liberalism*, London: Routledge.

Afterword

Giacomo Brioni

The main aim of the book was to bring forth the problem of foundation as one of the most important questions in modern and contemporary political philosophy. As the reader will have noticed, the identification of this problem is not dependent on the adoption of any particular approach or methodological standpoint. What changes is the language and set of categories used to articulate the question, but the essential contours of the latter remain the same. This explains the reason why the essays that have been presented here vary so widely in tone and scope – from pieces which draw from classical *loci* in the history of modern political thought (e.g., Scalone's and Bissiato's dialogue with Hobbes) and show considerable affinity with categories belonging to the "continental" tradition (the presence of Carl Schmitt in Scalone, Bissiato, and Monateri), all the way to contributions that hybridize philosophy with economic theory, and delve more into the late-twentieth-century debate originated from Rawls' theory (Marchetti and Brioni).

One could argue that the problem of foundation exerts its pressure even beyond Modernity. Every theoretical model of society, from Plato's *Republic* onwards, must confront the question of its actualization. That is to say: the search for stability is limited, on the one hand, by environmental factors (luck and necessity) and, on the other, by the heterogeneity of human wants, desires, and characters (here I draw freely on the observations of Strauss 1964 regarding Plato and Thucydides, but see also Portinaro 2023). However, it must also be acknowledged that foundationalism and its alternatives come to the foreground only at the beginning of Modernity, when notions of unity based on an external criterion of truth crumble under the weight of political and religious conflict. To use the key concepts in the title of Hirschman's (see 2013) famous synthesis of modern political thought, with Machiavelli politics becomes a matter of arranging the chaotic interplay of "passions" and "interests" in a way that keeps their destructive potential in check, while avoiding their complete repression.

The sets of ideas that are subsumed under the macro-categories of "liberalism" and "democracy" can all be seen as springing from this new basic view of political reality. Rights, constitutions, markets, elections, representation,

DOI: 10.4324/9781003471066-7

and so on are some of the tools which have been devised in order to produce the aforementioned combination of heterogeneity and unity. The essays in the present collection had the double function of highlighting the inner contradictions of these attempts to solve the problem of foundation, but also the fact that these contradictions are coeval with the problem itself. Every new approach, therefore, must be aware of its own fallibility or relative value. In a complex system, tweaking with one variable typically comes at a cost in some other feature – economic exchange vs. redistribution, freedom of participation vs. the need to exclude some acts which are detrimental to stability, concealing pluralism with the eventuality of conflict, and so on. As the debates that have been recalled in some of the present contributions have shown, it is not easy to achieve a definitive reconciliation of interests under the paradigm of liberal democracy, because even the meaning of its two components (liberalism and democracy) is difficult to ascertain and is the object of conflict. However, it is also necessary to understand whether this reconciliation can be attributed at all to the intentions of modern politics.

For the purposes of synthesis, we can identify two main *desiderata* of a foundational enterprise, or of a political order *lato sensu* – as they have emerged from the preceding essays. The first one is stability. A legal and political framework is a set of rules about what people can and cannot do. It identifies the available paths for individual choices by assigning (property) rights, and it delineates the rules for transactions. Whether this framework is interpreted as something that has evolved (the paradigm behind Marchetti's paper) or as a human construction (Brioni's public choice perspective), its main function is to regulate people's expectations. Since expectations are related to the available set of opportunities and to how information is distributed, a system of rules cannot avoid manipulating these objects in one way or another. Stability, therefore, is a function of procedural clarity: if rights are well defined, and if the rules for transactions are simple enough, people can project themselves, their plans of life, into the future. This is the conception that informs market institutions as a defining trait of the classical liberal option.

A similar function is associated with the mechanisms of political representation and democratic procedures. They are built to mediate between the need for the expression of people's different interests and the necessity of making decisions in a timely fashion. This means imposing a certain kind of homogeneity – such as the result of choices taken with the rule of simple majority – on the intrinsic plurality of the political community. The crucial point is that procedures allow single results to be overturned in order to experiment with different political solutions over time. In the liberal democratic framework, procedures that are fair and transparent ideally transfer these same properties to the outcomes, ensuring that order is publicly justifiable even to parties which are on the losing end of a particular play in the political game. Here stability means that political conflict is channeled into a system of impersonal rules, thus eliminating discretion from the picture. To the liberal democratic ideal, solid foundations are equal to the substitution of discretionary power, and the uncertainty that follows from it, with a constitutional environment which is not devised to favor any particular point of view over the others.

This is the crux of the matter for the constellation of post-foundational theories which Marchart (see 2007) analyzes. The constitutional or representative element in modern democracy inhibits the expression of claims by individuals and groups. In its attempts to create a shared conception of public reason based on rational consensus, liberal democracy obliterates those marginalized voices whose well-being depends on a radical questioning of existing institutions. As Mouffe (see 2013) emphasizes, liberal theories of justice are guilty of operating both a moralization and a rationalization of the political sphere. On the one hand, they assume that politics is the field of justification, namely the effort to attune the fabric of institutions to the moral perception of individuals; a successful order is one that is justifiable to every (reasonable) member of the community. On the other, liberalism (especially in the version coined by Habermas) aims to harmonize different conceptions of the good by means of rational discussion. Through deliberation, people are brought to identify their well-understood interest, as opposed to their selfish preferences. To the post-foundational theorist, both these approaches are different expressions of a single philosophical move: the attempt to evade the core of political action – that is, conflict – or to reframe it in terms belonging to other spheres of human life which seem more manageable or urbane.

By contrast, the paradigm of political difference assigns a fundamental role to the political. It does not try to neutralize it in any way. Rather, it confronts head on the fact that politics is resistant to the type of reasoning that takes grounding as its objective – strong causal and/or teleological thought. From a theoretical standpoint, this means that there exists no ultimate, natural spring of human order. Individual interactions are not directed to any single result, nor are they based on a definite set of anthropological motives. No particular list of rights can be assumed a priori, nor can we assert that everybody would agree on it once it is presented to them as the conclusion of sound reasoning. The fact that we expect our institutions to be stable does not guarantee that the latter possess logical consistency with some value judgment. Political life is based on conflict of interests, and contingent factors always play a role in how these conflicts are settled – time, relative advantage of the players, and so on. The image of unity we perceive in background structures is not an essential attribute, but something driven by utility or expediency. A momentary equilibrium cannot be "constitutionalized", that is, it cannot be transformed into a self-evident ontological principle. Post foundationalism aims to unearth the absence of ground under ordinary political interaction.

What is the operative meaning of these remarks for political theory? There is no univocal answer, and the variety of approaches this book includes is also a sign of this difficulty. Post-foundationalism is usually linked to theories of agonistic democracy. These perspectives identify (more or less straightforwardly) the political with conflict, and from this identification they infer the necessity for democracy to organize conflict through institutions. Democracy should be as open as possible because freedom is conditional on the possibility of participation to decision-making processes. In turn, participation is conditional on economic, social, and gender equality. Agonistic democracy explicitly calls for a redress of systemic injustices that are linked to the ideas of the Enlightenment and of liberal-capitalistic modernity. This paradigm also casts a suspicion on the integrity of current representative institutions. If representation is to work as a mediating device, it should reflect the real composition of claims in society, and it should not be captured by élite interests. The theory of agonistic democracy interprets the Schmittian concept of the political as a dynamic energy that underlies the formal institutions. The latter constitutes an ontological resistance to the former. Agonistic democracy can be seen as a plea for embedding some of the principles of revolution into democracy.

Though they do not take issue specifically with agonistic democracy, the first three contributions of the present volume articulate from different angles the conceptual horizon that characterizes it – not only in terms of theoretical standing but also in the way the history of political thought is understood. Both Scalone and Bissiato, together with Monateri's examination of the links between aesthetics and politics, seem to take Hobbes and Schmitt (together with Schmitt's interpretation of Hobbes) as the essential stepping stones for the genealogy of the question of foundation. Hobbes is the champion of foundationalism. His Commonwealth is the product of a human covenant. Although individuals are slaves to their passions (especially to the fear of violent death by the hands of others), they are ultimately able to recognize the need for order and to produce an artificial structure (the Leviathan) by a transfer of rights. In Schmitt's view, Hobbes acknowledges that the political – the friend/enemy distinction – is at the heart of the problem of order. However, he is also the first figure in the long process of neutralization, as his main objective is to do away with conflict and to guarantee the stability of peace. As Bissiato states, the sovereign in Hobbes' theory amounts to a representative mechanism, an entity that projects unity onto the political body, but can never grasp the full complexity of its empirical subjects. In turn, like in a game of mirrors, Schmitt himself looks at power not only in its anomic features but also in its ability to produce and maintain order. Be it as it may, the Schmittian concept of the political points directly to the friction between representation and reality. Democracy is built on the bet that this friction can be institutionalized without destructive consequences. Here Scalone and Bissiato depart from the Schmittian obsession over unity: political heterogeneity must be conceived as a liberating force. One the one hand (Scalone), it is misleading to speak of a "crisis" of democracy while referring to its governmental instability, because it is in the essence of democracy to reject any kind of monological principle of rule. "The people" cannot be conceived as a homogeneous entity, and popular sovereignty cannot be understood as an absolute or monopolistic power. "The people" is a manifold constellation of interests and associations that cannot be subsumed under any rigid structure, even if they enter into conflictual relationships. On the other (Bissiato), the modern theory of sovereignty has often overlooked the element of the body. As the Foucaultian and Feminist analysis of power structures has pointed out, the body is something government has always tried to discipline. However, there is an irreducible element of dynamism, of empirical reality, that cannot be controlled by sovereignty.

As the reader will have noticed, Brioni and Marchetti's papers take a different route *vis-a-vis* the post-foundational construction. They both start by comparing the latter's fundamental tenets with the ones belonging to economic theory and contemporary social science. With respect to the normativistic liberal framework, the results are similar. In either case, it emerges that notions of public reason, rational/reasonable consensus on principles, and moral community are too *naive* or thin and do not take into account the real interplay of human interests. There is, however, a decisive matter in which economic reasoning supplements post-foundational discourse, perhaps with more theoretical clarity: the analysis of actual human behavior in order to better understand institutional equilibria. Depending on which incentive structure is superimposed on individual actions, people are more prone to conflict, voluntary cooperation, or negotiation. However, against constructivism, one should not look at political order as something springing from human will. In turn, institutions are reinforced or eroded by the complex network of beliefs and practices in which people engage day by day. As Marchetti recalls by drawing on neo-institutionalist categories, informal rules are just as important as formal structures. Therefore, a political philosophy that is truly post-foundational needs to be completed by experimental work about how individuals and groups fare in different institutional environments. This is important in order to judge the import of trade-offs such as the one between stability of order and political change, between private and collective action, and so on.

In conclusion, it is the polyphonic approach taken up in the course of this volume that seems to be most promising with regard to the problem of foundation. Even if methods do not always agree in their implications, and normative conclusions sometimes clash, the recurring features of the field of inquiry guarantee a baseline from which dialogue can begin. As an example, one need only recall that, although Rawls is credited with the rebirth of political philosophy in the '70s, he wasn't building his ideas about liberal democracy in a vacuum. Behind and aside him stood the intense activity of welfare economists, decision theorists, and political scientists, who were delving in a similar way into the general question of social organization. The picture here is similar. We are not dealing with a problem that is a province of one particular discipline: everyone who seeks to understand how people live together needs to confront the problem of foundation, or, in other words, of order and social change.

Bibliography

Hirschman, A.O. (2013) *The Passions and the Interests: Political Arguments in Favor of Capitalism Before Its Triumph*, Princeton: Princeton University Press.

Marchart, O. (2007) *Post-Foundational Political Thought: Political Difference in Nancy, Lefort, Badiou and Laclau*, Edinburgh: Edinburgh University Press.

Mouffe, C. (2013) *Hegemony, Radical Democracy, and the Political*, ed. by James Martin, London: Routledge.

Portinaro, P.P. (2023) *Il realismo politico: Nuova edizione ampliata*, Brescia: Scholè.

Strauss, L. (1964) *The City and Man*, Chicago and London: The University of Chicago Press.

Index

Kolibri 360 GmbH
Ferdinand-Jühlke-Straße 7
99095 Erfurt, Deutschland
produktsicherheit@kolibri360.de